"Caren Baruch-Feldman has synthesized a masterful workbook that will prepare young people to thrive in both good and challenging times. There are so many books written for adults on how to shape teens. Finally, here is one written for youth in a respectful, understandable, *actionable* tone that inherently recognizes young people as experts in their own lives who will take the reins when offered the tools to become their best selves. *Bravo.*"

—**Kenneth Ginsburg, MD, MS-Ed**, author of *Building Resilience in Children and Teens* and *Raising Kids to Thrive*

"As a forty-year, veteran educator that has worked with Angela Duckworth since she was in graduate school, I am pleased to endorse *The Grit Guide for Teens*. Baruch-Feldman incorporates strategies such as flow charts, goal setting, sentence completion, and self-reflection and writing exercises that will engage teenagers, and lead them to self-discovery and growth. *The Grit Guide for Teens* is an essential tool for educators, parents, and anyone seeking to better grasp and assist young people in their path to success."

—**David Meketon**, school research liaison to Duckworth Lab in the department of psychology at the University of Pennsylvania

"Today's world is filled with stress and pressure—acutely felt by many teens. Caren Baruch-Feldman has written a truly remarkable book that provides teens with realistic and practical strategies for managing challenging situations and developing perseverance, grit, and resilience. Baruch-Feldman's empathy for the world experienced by teens and her clinical acumen, warmth, and humor are apparent throughout this book. In addition, her online recommendations for parents and teachers to nurture grit in adolescents serve as a wonderful resource."

—**Robert Brooks, PhD**, faculty member at Harvard Medical School, and coauthor of *Raising Resilient Children*

"Everywhere teens look, they are facing seeming catastrophes. This book is a much-needed guide to navigate the tumultuous emotional waters of youth. Caren Baruch-Feldman offers a highly creative, versatile conception of grit—one that can help teenagers step up to life and fully realize their possibilities!"

—**Scott Barry Kaufman**, scientific director at the Imagination Institute at the University of Pennsylvania and author of *Ungifted*

"A must-have for teens and their parents. Simple, elegant, scientifically-proven, and practical."

—**Braco Pobric**, author of *Habits and Happiness*

"Caren Baruch-Feldman does an excellent job of taking the latest research on grit and turning it into an accessible, user-friendly workbook for teens—the very people who can benefit most from a boost in grit and resilience."

—**Donna Stokes**, executive editor for *Live Happy* magazine

"How do you turn knowledge into skills, and skills into life? How do you find and grab the knowledge you need when you need it? In *The Grit Guide for Teens*, Caren Baruch-Feldman is funneling important information about grit and how to build it to adolescents, their parents, and teachers. The *why*, the *what*, and the *how* of grit is the scaffold for this important story about how to build a life of passion, persistence, and purpose, developing skills that will help teens (and anyone) to navigate life in all its glory—chaos, opportunity, trouble and luck! In increasingly uncertain times, building a strong inner life and a healthy psychological core will help. *The Grit Guide for Teens* is gold!"

—**Gabrielle Kelly**, director of the Wellbeing and Resilience Centre at the South Australian Health and Medical Research Institute

"Teens today—more than ever—need to think about the long-term, persevere in the face of setbacks, and grow from their mistakes. Caren Baruch-Feldman's *The Grit Guide for Teens* provides a road map to help teens meet the challenges of today's competitive world. *The Grit Guide for Teens* has taken the latest research in the fields of cognitive behavioral therapy (CBT), behavior change, and grit, and has made it accessible. This skills-building approach will help teens learn to grow psychologically. St. John's University and The Albert Ellis Institute are proud to include Baruch-Feldman as one of their graduates. *The Grit Guide for Teens* is a must-have for today's teens and the individuals who care about them."

—**Ray DiGiuseppe, PhD, ABPP**, professor and chair of the department of psychology at St. John's University, past president of the Association for Behavioral and Cognitive Therapies, and director of professional education at The Albert Ellis Institute

"Caren Baruch-Feldman has packed a lot of research, worksheets, and practical information into this important and timely book. Research shows that grit is considered the key to success, and having this workbook during the formative teen years could positively impact the rest of a person's life."

—**Caroline Adams Miller, MAPP**, author of *Getting Grit* and *My Name is Caroline*, and coauthor of *Creating Your Best Life*

"Just when you thought gritty kids were an endangered species, Caren Baruch-Feldman delivers a concise and engaging guide to teenage happiness. That's right, brooding and complaining are not the default teenage mindsets. Success comes from perseverance, and Baruch-Feldman writes the ideal prescription. Drawing on scientific research without sounding stuffy for a second, Baruch-Feldman shares her winning formula through interviews with real teens, exercises for the reader, and goals that extend far beyond the pages of the workbook. Buy this book for every teen you know and watch inspiration turn to effort, skill, and achievement!"

> —**Christopher Thurber, PhD, ABPP**, psychologist at Phillips Exeter Academy, coauthor of *The Summer Camp Handbook*, and cofounder of www.expertonlinetraining.com

"*The Grit Guide for Teens* is fabulous. This inspirational guide provides very practical and accessible information and activities for teens that are underpinned by rigorous, up-to-date psychological research. The book provides a sound evidence base for what works best to facilitate teens' psychological well-being and resilience. The step-by-step strategies in this book will make it easy for teens to apply these important concepts in their own lives, and are written in a style that will appeal to both teens and adults."

> —**Toni Noble, PhD**, adjunct professor at the Institute for Positive Psychology & Education at Australian Catholic University, and coauthor of *Bounce Back!*

"Success—however we define it—requires the ability to persist when the going gets tough. So does overcoming almost any kind of adversity. *The Grit Guide for Teens* is easy to read, and shows you how to become more persistent, successful, and resilient with whatever you set out to do in life."

> —**Mark Bertin, MD**, developmental pediatrician and author of *Mindful Parenting for ADHD* and *How Children Thrive*

"Persistence-perseverance-grit: from my perspective it is when purpose and practice transform desire into accomplishment. Caren Baruch-Feldman has created an excellent workbook that can help every young person become more skilled and focused, and every educator and parent more intentional and motivated."

> —**Gil G. Noam, PhD, EdD**, faculty member at Harvard Medical School, and founder and director of The PEAR Institute: Partnerships in Education and Resilience, at Harvard University

"Grit expert Caren Baruch-Feldman has created an engaging, interesting, and helpful workbook for teens who want to transform their passions and talents into true skills. *The Grit Guide for Teens* seamlessly incorporates current research on grit, developing optimism, growth mind-set, good habits, gratitude, and self-control—and creates step-by-step instructions that make understanding this complex research accessible and fun. As a school psychologist, I can see myself working through these chapters with my students, individually or in groups, to their great benefit. I look forward to counting on *The Grit Guide for Teens* to help my students learn invaluable lessons about themselves and growing their grit in order to achieve their goals."

> —**Rebecca Comizio, MA-Ed, MA**, nationally certified school psychologist (NCSP)

"As high school educators, we have always been interested in our students' investment in their learning, and not just in the quality of their work output. We speak often about grit as an integral habit of mind, but we are never quite certain how to instill and inspire it within our students. Caren Baruch-Feldman has given teenagers and those of us charged to work with them an invaluable and accessible tool with which we might all self-reflect and grow. *The Grit Guide for Teens* is a breakthrough."

> —**Mark Shinar, EdD**, director of general studies at SAR High School

"*The Grit Guide for Teens* is a comprehensive, exciting, and—most importantly—*fun* guide for young people to help them develop resilience skills in the face of an increasingly stressful and anxiety-ridden world. Baruch-Feldman delves into current research on grit and positive psychology, speaks to teenagers at their level, and engages them using their language and interests. I would highly recommend this book to any teen who crosses my path."

> —**Elizabeth Wright**, Paralympic medalist and cofounder of the character education program at Resilience Wellbeing Success

"As teens coming out of high school, this book is absolutely a must-read! Working on it with Caren Baruch-Feldman has not only taught us about grit, but more about ourselves than we could have ever imagined. For any teen with any struggle, it is the ultimate recipe for success, with tools for conquering common obstacles like self-control, pessimism, and giving up. This book is truly life changing!"

> —**Kira Cohen** and **Katie Parker**, recent graduates from SAR High School

the
grit guide
for teens

a workbook to help you build
perseverance, self-control
& a growth mindset

CAREN BARUCH-FELDMAN, PhD

Instant Help Books
An Imprint of New Harbinger Publications, Inc.

Publisher's Note

This publication is designed to provide accurate and authoritative information in regard to the subject matter covered. It is sold with the understanding that the publisher is not engaged in rendering psychological, financial, legal, or other professional services. If expert assistance or counseling is needed, the services of a competent professional should be sought.

Distributed in Canada by Raincoast Books

Copyright © 2017 by Caren Baruch-Feldman
     Instant Help Books
     An Imprint of New Harbinger Publications, Inc.
     5674 Shattuck Avenue
     Oakland, CA 94609
     www.newharbinger.com

Cover design by Amy Shoup

Acquired by Melissa Valentine

Edited by Kristi Hein

All Rights Reserved

Library of Congress Cataloging-in-Publication Data on file

19 18 17

10 9 8 7 6 5 4 3 2 1   First Printing

In memory of my father, Marcel Baruch, who was gritty before it was trendy.

Contents

contents

Foreword

Caren Baruch-Feldman's *Grit Guide for Teens* fills a real need. Its unique mix of research and common sense makes for an enjoyable, educational, and inviting book that I believe will help young people, parents, and educators for years to come. From the Neanderthal days to now, grit has always been an integral factor in people's success—but maybe, just maybe, it is even more important today than ever before.

After defining *grit* with the work of Angela Duckworth and other researchers, Caren puts it in down-to-earth terms and uses real-life examples that will actually resonate with teenagers. She isn't just describing the hurdles at West Point or the pain felt by marathon runners. She writes about the grit needed in gym class and writing the Harry Potter series.

I was particularly struck by the division into five distinct grit domains: academic grit, social/relationship grit, wellness/health grit, extracurricular grit, and emotional grit. In the same way that Howard Gardner recognized that we are more or less successful in different situations because we pull from distinct multiple intelligences, Caren illustrates how our grit will vary depending upon the context in which we find ourselves. Some of us will be grittier on an academic task, while others will most readily use grit in a social setting. As Caren explains, understanding how grit can vary due to situation and context is the first step in developing grit.

There has been a great deal of writing and talk about grit, and while most people seem to appreciate its power, there are also questions of how grit can be instilled and developed. This book offers good ideas and hands-on strategies. From interactive surveys that cause teens to reflect on their situations, attitudes, and behaviors to specific examples and models to overcome obstacles, the *Grit Guide for Teens* helps teens and their parents become more insightful and proactive at using grit to solve problems in their day-to-day lives. I suspect that even the most reluctant teenager— *Who needs grit? Not me!* —will find this book interesting and helpful.

Caren's bias is clear: grit is an important part of problem-solving, and we can all develop more grit. This book is a useful tool to do just that!

—Thomas R. Hoerr, PhD
Emeritus Head of School, New City School; St. Louis, MO
Author of *The Formative Five: Fostering Grit, Empathy, and Other Success Skills Every Student Needs*

Introduction

I do not think that there is any other quality so essential to success of any kind as the quality of perseverance. It overcomes almost everything, even nature.

—John D. Rockefeller

Welcome to the *Grit Guide for Teens*. You may be wondering, what is grit? Why is grit important? Why do I need it? How will this workbook help me get it?

Grit is the ability to stick with things that are important to you. It's viewing obstacles as challenges to overcome rather than reasons to quit. In sum, grit is the ability to accomplish, in the face of setbacks or challenges, the long-term goals that are important to *you*. Having grit will help you study for a final exam that's two weeks away or keep you from quitting a sport after a tough game. It's what forces you to face a difficult emotion or uncomfortable feeling so you can emerge feeling stronger and more resilient. In short, grit is an essential ingredient to achieving your goals, no matter what they might be.[1]

As a teen growing up today, you might find it difficult to have grit. You are at an age when failure can seem crushing. When you lose a game or flunk a test, it might feel like the end of the world. The pressure and stakes are high, and you have to balance the demands of school, extracurricular activities, and family obligations. You are often asked to do things you just don't want to do. And if those pressures weren't enough, there is so much to distract and discourage you—from social media to peer pressure. With all of these pressures, it can be especially hard to set long-term goals and find the strength to accomplish them—unless you have *grit*.

That's where this workbook comes in. This workbook includes step-by-step instructions on how to develop grit and incorporate it into your life. Grit has traditionally been applied to academics and areas of elite performance like athletics or music, but this workbook will show you how grit can also help you to improve your relationships, wellness, and emotional well-being. Grit can be developed, like any other skill, when it is broken down into steps and applied to specific areas where grit is essential: academics, social relationships, health and wellness, extracurricular activities, and emotional well-being.

Through the activities in chapter 1, you will learn what grit is, determine your current level of grit, and identify the area in which you would like to become grittier (your *grit goal*). In chapter 2, you'll find out how to recognize and confront the irrational thoughts that are getting in your way and develop new ways of thinking that will promote a grittier mind-set. In chapter 3, you will turn those thoughts into action by learning strategies that have been found to strengthen stick-to-it-iveness and build gritty behavior. In chapter 4, you will find ways to overcome barriers to grit so that you can push through when the going gets tough. The strategies you will learn are based on my experience as a cognitive-behavioral psychologist as well as emerging research in the field of positive psychology. My goal for you is to see the benefit of focusing on the long term and to embrace the struggle that comes with being a teen, because in that struggle lies the possibility for real growth.

Writing this workbook required real grit on my part. I had to constantly remind myself of my long-term goal of finishing the book so that I wouldn't get sidetracked by short-term temptations like watching the *Real Housewives* on television! There were many obstacles along the way, like feeling discouraged by the many edits and rewrites and having to get up at 5 a.m. to write, but I tried to see those challenges as part of the process. I am hopeful that this workbook will be as rewarding for you as writing it was for me.

Wishing you much success on your journey.

Dr. Caren Baruch-Feldman

P.S. If you're a parent, teacher or counselor, check out the chapters I've written on what *you* can do to increase a teen's grit. They're available for you to download at http://www.newharbinger.com/38563.

CHAPTER 1

Understanding Grit: Grit 101

No grit, no pearl.

—Anonymous

In this chapter, you'll learn:

1. What grit is and why it's important for your success.

2. How gritty you are overall and within the different areas/domains of your life.

3. Where your grit is already strong and where it needs to grow.

4. The formula for grit.

5. How a positive approach can help you grow your grit.

Let's get started!

1 what is grit?

A river cuts through rock, not because of its power, but because of its persistence.

—Jim Watkins

for you to know

Imagine talented young men and women competing in the Scripps National Spelling Bee. All of the contestants were bright, but who made it to the winner's circle?

Imagine West Point Cadets, all strong and capable, but some were more successful than others at surviving the grueling summer training program known as "Beast Barracks."

In both cases, it wasn't talent or IQ that made the difference. It was *grit*.

At the Spelling Bee, the contestants with the most grit were the ones who advanced to the finals, not because they were smarter or naturally better spellers, but because they had *studied and practiced* more than the others.[2]

For the cadets, grit mattered more than intelligence, leadership ability, or physical fitness. The cadets with grit *just did not quit*. They completed the challenging training at higher rates than their less gritty peers.[3]

What Is Grit?

The quality of grit—as specifically described by psychologist, author, and leading expert in this field, Angela Duckworth—is "passion and perseverance for long-term and meaningful goals."[4] This kind of passion is not about intense emotions or infatuation. It's about having direction and commitment. Grit is the ability to stay focused on achieving your long-term goals. It's about sticking with the things that are important to you—like working on a project for a long period of time or pursuing a sport over many years. When you have this kind of passion, you are able to stay committed to a task that may be difficult or boring.

Grit is also about perseverance. To persevere means to stick with it; to continue working hard even after experiencing difficulty or failure. Perseverance is keeping up with your training even after you've been cut from the team—so you can try out again next year. Perseverance is bouncing back after a social encounter doesn't go your way. It means knowing every encounter (good or bad) gets you closer to your ultimate goal of having more friendships.

It is when you combine these two qualities—passion and perseverance—over the long term that you realize all the benefits associated with grit.

Why Is Grit Important?

Grit is important because it allows you to use passion and perseverance to transform talent into skill. Although talent is important, without effort or grit, talent is nothing more than unmet potential. It is only with effort that talent becomes a skill that leads to success. While talent is important, effort is doubly important—as Duckworth depicts in this equation[5]:

Grit = Effort

Talent x Effort (grit) = Skill

Skill x Effort (grit) = Achievement

For example, you may have talent as a comedian, but in order to turn that talent into a skill you need to work at it consistently (grit). When you work on your routines (for example, trying out jokes, practicing in front of a mirror), you get better, which leads to success. Comedians like Jimmy Fallon, Amy Schumer, and Jerry Seinfeld don't just have talent; they continually use their talent to practice and refine their skills.

Let's hear what some teens have to say about what grit means to them and why it is important.

"In gym class, we start off each class with core work like planks and crunches. The rest of the class would complain and not participate, but I adopted an attitude that I loved core exercises and I was able to improve that way. I think what made me so gritty and able to stick with the class was that I knew doing those exercises would eventually lead to having a fit, toned, healthy body."

—Nia, high school senior

"When I was in high school, I got sick and missed a lot of school. I felt like I didn't know what was going on with my friends, and I fell behind in my classes. When I got better, I really wanted to switch schools. But I feel like I showed grit because I did go back to my old school. And, although some of my friendships had changed, I found out who my true friends were. Now I am in college and I know that whatever obstacle I might face, I will be able to bounce back."

—Lindsey, college freshman

"When I was growing up, my mom didn't like seeing me upset. Whenever I was angry or sad, she stepped in to fix things. I know she was trying to help, but I wish she would have let me experience my feelings and problems. When I got older, I didn't feel prepared for life's ups and downs. I have worked hard to get grittier, and now I am able to face challenges head on and not give up. Having a grittier outlook is not always easy, but I know it will help me in the long run."

—Maurice, college sophmore

We just heard from some teens. Now, let's hear from *you*.

for you to do

1. What does grit mean to you? Can you define grit in your own words?

   _____

2. Why is grit important to you?

   _____

3. Write about a time when you exhibited grit by sticking with something difficult. What do you think led to that success?

   _____

4. Write about a time that you weren't so gritty and gave up on something prematurely. How did it make you feel?

   _____

5. When you persevered with a challenging task despite failure or difficulty, did you feel the hard work and sacrifice was worth it?

   Yes ☐   Not yet* ☐

6. If you answered not yet, what might have helped you feel like it was worth it?

   _____

---

* Borrowing a concept from psychologist Carol Dweck,[6] I have purposely made the responses *yes* or *not yet* instead of *yes* or *no* to help you see that being gritty is a process and that you are on a journey of growth!

let's dig deeper

Think about someone who has successfully achieved an important long-term goal and ask him or her the following questions. If it's someone you don't know, you can think about how the person might answer.

1. Ask or think about the goal and what helped the person to achieve success.

2. Ask or think about whether the person succeeded on pure talent alone.

3. Ask or think about whether the person had setbacks and struggles. How did he or she deal with the obstacles faced?

4. Would you describe this individual as gritty?

Sometimes we see accomplished people and do not realize all the hard work that went into their achievement. For example, we might think of the success of the Harry Potter books, but not about the hours J.K. Rowling spent writing in obscurity before hitting the best seller list. We are often told that Isaac Newton discovered gravity by being hit on the head by an apple; in fact, he spent thousands of hours investigating gravity. Success isn't a matter of just talent or luck; it takes stick-to-itiveness, hard work, and a determination to overcome challenges—all parts of every successful person's road to success.

But even though grit is important, it is also important to know when to adjust your goals and expectations when the original goals prove too difficult or you have lost interest in the task. Having grit doesn't mean never quitting, but when you decide to quit, you do it thoughtfully, not just because things have gotten hard. My objective for *you* is to be in charge of your fate and accomplish the goals you have set for yourself because they are important to you.

Now that you know what grit is and why it is important, let's find out how gritty you are.

2 how much grit do I have?

Over time, grit is what separates fruitful lives from aimlessness.

—John Ortberg

for you to know

In this activity, you can find out how gritty you are right *now*. By assessing your current level of grit, as well as identifying areas where you currently are demonstrating grit, you can learn from your strengths in order to overcome your weaknesses.

Don't worry if your current grit level is low. Grit can be learned! Although grit can be hampered by circumstances like genetics, poverty, stress, or even extreme wealth, no matter your circumstances, you *can* get to the top of your potential *range* and become grittier.[7]

for you to do

Grit Survey

Please complete this survey now and again when you have finished the workbook. Although change takes time, I am confident that by working through the activities your grit will grow.

1. Do you think you have grit—the ability to stick with long-term goals and bounce back from failure or challenges?

1	2	3	4	5
Never	Rarely	Sometimes	Often	Always

2. Do you stick to long-term goals and finish what you started?

1	2	3	4	5
Never	Rarely	Sometimes	Often	Always

3. Can you bounce back from setbacks or challenges?

1	2	3	4	5
Never	Rarely	Sometimes	Often	Always

4. Are you able to think about what will feel good in the long run and not just what feels good in the moment?

1	2	3	4	5
Never	Rarely	Sometimes	Often	Always

5. Do you have grit when it comes to **schoolwork**? For example, can you persist and overcome challenges when it comes to papers, tests, or homework?

1	2	3	4	5
Never	Rarely	Sometimes	Often	Always

6. Are you gritty in **social situations** and with **relationships**? For example, when you have a problem with a friend, can you face the problem and work things out? Are you able to deal with challenging social situations?

1	2	3	4	5
Never	Rarely	Sometimes	Often	Always

7. Are you gritty about your **health and wellness**? For example, are you able to maintain an exercise routine, sleep schedule, and healthy eating habits? Can you get back on track when your routine breaks down?

1	2	3	4	5
Never	Rarely	Sometimes	Often	Always

8. Are you gritty in **extracurricular activities** like sports and the arts? Are you able to practice, persist, and rebound from failure?

1	2	3	4	5
Never	Rarely	Sometimes	Often	Always

9. Are you gritty **emotionally**? Are you able to cope effectively when you feel down, worried, or angry? Do you face your fears rather than avoid them?

1	2	3	4	5
Never	Rarely	Sometimes	Often	Always

Write down your answer to question 1 (your overall grit level) here. We will refer back to this at the end of the book. _____

In the next activity, we will take a look at different areas of teenage life—what I call *grit domains* (the items in **bold** in the survey). These domains were selected because they are most relevant to your life as a teenager. We'll explore the areas in which you are already gritty (your *grit strengths*) and the ones where you want your grit to grow (your *grit goal*).

3 where do I need to be grittier?

*Winners evaluate themselves in a positive manner and look
for their strengths as they work to overcome weaknesses.*

—Zig Ziglar

for you to know

Most of us aren't gritty in every situation; our grit level depends on the activity or circumstance.[8] For example, I have always been gritty academically: getting good grades in school, succeeding professionally. But until recently, I had a hard time sticking to a diet and exercise plan.

In this activity, I will ask you to identify an area(s) of your life where you are already displaying grit (your grit strengths) and an area/domain where you want to be grittier (your grit goal). My goal is for you to learn from your own strengths as well as acquire new skills to address your weaknesses.

We will be exploring five grit domains in this workbook:

1. *Academic Grit*—Having academic grit allows you to persevere in tasks like papers, tests, and homework and helps you fulfill your academic responsibilities over the long haul.

2. *Social/Relationship Grit*—Social/relationship grit helps you put yourself in social situations that you want to take on even when you feel uncomfortable. It's not about turning an introvert into an extrovert, but rather accomplishing social/ relationship goals that are important to each person.

3. *Wellness/Health Grit*—Having wellness/health grit helps you stick to an exercise routine, sleep schedule, or maintain healthy eating habits. When you hit a challenge in this area, you are able to get back on track.

4. *Extracurricular Grit*—With extracurricular grit, you are able to practice, persist, and rebound when faced with obstacles or setbacks in extracurricular activities like sports, the arts, or volunteering.

5. *Emotional Grit*—Emotional grit helps you manage your emotions, face your fears, cope with anger, and recover from emotional challenges. With emotional grit, you are able to control your emotions instead of letting them control you.

Let's see what Lisa's grit strengths and weaknesses are.

Lisa's Story

Lisa, a high school senior, rated her grittiness in each domain on a scale of 1 (the lowest) to 5 (the highest). As you can see, Lisa is not gritty across all categories. Like everyone, she has strengths and weaknesses when it comes to grit.

Academic Grit	Social/Relationship Grit	Wellness/Health Grit	Extracurricular Grit	Emotional Grit
Strength = 5	Weakness = 1	Depends on the area = 3	Pretty strong = 4	Depends on the area = 2
"I can persist on difficult school-related tasks and feel passionate about my schoolwork. When I don't do well on a test, I go to the teacher to figure out how to improve."	"My social/relationship grit is less developed. Although I want to be more social, if I go to a party and feel uncomfortable, I leave."	"In terms of eating and sleeping, I am quite gritty, but not so much with exercise. I say I'm going to run, but I never do."	"I play violin. I practice regularly and have improved over the years."	"I can handle it when I don't do well at school. I know I can make it up next time. But I worry a lot about speaking in front of the class. I panic when I know I have to talk in front of everyone."

for you to do

Using Lisa as an example, think about your own grit strengths and weaknesses. Rate each domain on a scale from 1 (the lowest, or your weakness) to 5 (the highest, or your strength). You don't have to assign a different number for every domain; you may want to give two areas the same rating. When you've finished rating yourself, write a little about your strengths and weaknesses like Lisa did.

Academic Grit	Social/ Relationship Grit	Wellness/ Health Grit	Extracurricular Grit	Emotional Grit
Rating = _____	Rating = _____	Rating = _____	Rating = _____	Rating = _____

let's dig deeper

In what domain are you already showing grit?

_____

_____

Write down some ways you are thinking and behaving in this domain that you think helps you be so gritty.

_____

_____

_____

You may have noticed that your grit strength is in an area that is important to you. You might even feel confident in this area. When you face challenges in this area, you feel like you can overcome them successfully. This is no coincidence!

By thinking more deeply about your grit strength, you will be able to apply what you are doing in that area to the area in which you are less gritty.

What domain are you interested in improving? _____

This will be your grit goal for this workbook.

Your grit goal doesn't have to be in the area with the lowest score. It can be in an area where you have identified a weakness and *where it is important for you to improve.* The important part of picking a goal is that you are committed to achieving it and it is meaningful to you.

For example, Lisa might select "social/relationship grit" as her grit goal. This domain is her weakest area and one she is motivated to improve. She might instead have selected "wellness/health grit" or "emotional grit" because she has room to grow in those domains too.

You may also have noticed that there can be overlap among the domains. For example, improving your grit in terms of running could fall under either the extra-curricular or the wellness/health domain. It is not important which domain you select as long as you are committed to your grit goal.

Keep your primary grit goal in mind as you complete the activities in this workbook. If you'd like to improve in more than one domain, feel free to go through the activities again.

The goal of this workbook is for you to:

- Learn from your strengths.

- Find a way to feel passionate about the area in which you want to improve.

- Feel confident in your ability to succeed.

- Behave in ways that lead to success.

- Reduce the barriers to your success.

All of this points to a winning formula for grit. Read on to learn what really goes into grit!

4 your formula for grit

I like things to happen. And if they don't happen, I like to make them happen.

—Winston Churchill

for you to know

In the previous activities, you (1) learned what grit is and why it is important, (2) discovered how gritty you are now, and (3) identified your grit strengths and grit goal. Now it's time to learn the *formula* for grit. How can *you* become grittier?

The formula contains *why* you might choose to act gritty and *how* to do it.

Why You Choose to Be Gritty (your mind-set or motivation):

- You believe in the *benefit or importance* of your goal.

- You believe that the *effort or cost* needed to achieve your goal is worth it.

- You believe that the *likelihood of achieving* your goal is high.[9]

For example, if you are academically gritty, then you believe in the *value and importance* of school, you believe that the *costs* of doing your schoolwork consistently are worth it, and you are *confident* in your ability to succeed academically. This is the *why*.

How to Become Grittier (your volition or behavior)

It is not enough to have the right motivation or mind-set. You also need the *behavior* to turn your motivation into action. This is the *how*. For example, you can't just be motivated to be a better tennis player—you need to get on the courts and practice. It is only when your motivation (the why) is combined with action (the how) that real success occurs.

So here is the formula:

$$\text{Motivation (mind-set)} + \text{Volition (behavior)} = \text{Success}^{10}$$

This formula, focusing on both mind-set (the why) + behavior (the how), is the focus of this workbook.

for you to do

In the following example, underline the key phrases that indicate (1) the importance of Kevin's goal, (2) the costs that may be involved, and (3) the likelihood of Kevin's achieving his goal. Also, indicate where you see Kevin's *motivation* and the *behavior* that supports his goal.

Kevin is gritty about karate. Karate is important to Kevin because it makes him feel good and provides stress relief. The dojo membership is expensive, but the cost seems worth it because Kevin likes the results he is getting and feels confident that he can improve. Kevin tries to go to class on a regular basis. He finds that when he goes on his own, it is harder for him to feel motivated, so he often makes plans to go with friends.

In the next example, circle the key phrases that may be contributing to Sara's *lack of grit*.

Sara wants to be grittier about her piano playing. She likes to play because she loves music, but she doesn't really like to practice. Her progress seems slow, and she can't play the songs her sister is playing. She plays just enough to fill out the weekly practice chart her teacher gives her.

Kevin's calculations within the formula add up when it comes to Karate—he's motivated, he finds the personal cost reasonable, and he's confident in his success. For Sara, however, the calculations don't add up. She has the motivation, but she's not backing it up with gritty behavior. Although piano is important to her, both the costs and the likelihood of her success are working against her.

let's dig deeper

Now try the formula on yourself.

Keeping your grit goal in mind, ask yourself these questions:

1. Is this goal important to me? What are the benefits?

   _____

2. What is my motivation for achieving this goal? Why does it matter to me?

   _____

3. How likely is it that I will achieve my goal?

   _____

4. What are the personal costs associated with pursuing my goal? (Research indicates that we are super sensitive to "costs" or "losses." Therefore, this question is especially important to address.)[11]

   _____

5. Is there a way to reduce these personal costs?

   _____

6. What behaviors am I practicing to support my goal?

   _____

In the next activity, you will learn how to connect to your grit goal in a positive way and make grit matter.

5   making grit matter

When we are no longer able to change a situation—
we are challenged to change ourselves.

—Viktor Frankl

for you to know

As you saw in activity 4, it is easier to be gritty about a task that is important to you, where the personal costs are low, and where there is a high likelihood that you will succeed. (That was probably the case for your current area of grit strength.) But it can be much harder to feel passion for something that you don't find initially interesting or motivating. It is also hard to persevere with something that is very challenging for you or where the personal costs seem too high.

What do you do then?

If you can find the positive in your grit goal—or make it about *yes*—you will be able to persevere even when there are aspects you may not feel excited about right now.

To see why it is important to develop grit from a more positive place, try doing this exercise with me.

First, shake your head no. How does that make you feel?

Now nod your head yes. How did that feel?

If you are like most people, when you shook your head no, you might have felt the muscles in your face tighten, and felt an increase in negative emotions and even a tendency to take a step back.

However, nodding your head yes is often accompanied by feelings of peace, acceptance, and lightness.[12]

So what does this have to do with developing grit? We often try to be gritty by telling ourselves no—no more wasting time with social media, no more cake, no more feeling anxious. However, when we focus on the no, we often make things harder for ourselves. If we can instead focus on the yes—the positive benefits of changing a behavior—it will be easier to persevere and overcome setbacks. I can identify with this personally. In the past, whenever I had tried to lose weight, it was always from a place of no—what I had to give up in order to lose weight. This time, I focused on what I considered the positive aspects of losing weight: feeling healthier, having more energy, and being able to wear clothes I like that were already in my closet. This attitude is helpful not just for weight loss. Whether it's getting yourself to manage your time, reaching out to new friends, playing a sport, or sticking with a difficult assignment, when you can think about these tasks in a positive way—in terms of what you'll gain, and how satisfied you'll feel for making an effort—they become easier to accomplish.

here are some ways to make it about yes!

Look for Control and/or Choice Over the Activity

If you play an instrument, for example, it can help to have a say in who your teacher is, the type of music you play, or how often you perform. Having some kind of control can help foster intrinsic motivation, which means performing an activity for its own sake rather than to earn a reward or avoid a punishment.[13]

Aim for the "Goldilocks Level"

See if you can create tasks that are at the "Goldilocks level"—that is, not too easy and not too hard but just right.[14] This is especially important when you are starting out, because the goal might seem too hard at first. Try breaking down a large goal into smaller goals that you can manage but that aren't so easy that you'll never see progress. We'll talk more about setting goals in activity 13.

See How the Behavior Fits into a Larger Goal You Might Find Important

Maybe you'd like to be grittier in your extracurricular activities, but practicing for a piano recital is getting tedious. Or maybe you're trying to be grittier in school, but you don't see the point of memorizing chemistry formulas. See if you can connect these small, less important goals to a larger, more important goal. Ask yourself: *Am I willing to accept this tradeoff—doing something I don't want to do now, so I can reach a larger goal that is important to me?* For example, thinking about the larger goal—performing well at the concert, getting into the college of your dreams, or maybe even getting your parents off your back—might be the *yes!* that can help motivate you.

Tie Your Current Actions to a Core Value

Core values guide our motivation and actions because we want to live up to them.[15] For example, maybe you don't want to babysit now that your friends asked you to go out. How can you be gritty in keeping this commitment? Tie it to a core value that is important to you, like being *caring* or *responsible*. Ask yourself: would a caring and responsible person back out of the job? Connecting the behavior to a core value might help you find the motivation you need. (We will talk more about values in activity 19.)

Connect the Task to a Higher Sense of Purpose

Try seeing how the behavior might be meaningful not only to you, but to the world at large. Ask yourself: *How can this activity make a positive contribution to others?* If your actions might not only help you but also help others, you are more likely to be persistent even with tasks you find tedious or challenging.[16] (We will also talk more about purpose in activity 19.)

Let's look at Ryan's story and see how he made it about yes!

Ryan's Story

Ryan works in an elementary school cafeteria. The pay isn't great, and it can be noisy, but Ryan has learned to tap into his core values of caring and connecting. He doesn't think about the mess or the noise; instead, he focuses on being helpful and bringing a smile to everyone's face. In this way, Ryan has connected his job to a "higher purpose."

for you to do

Keep your grit goal in mind as you answer the following questions.

1. Can you frame it in the positive?

   Yes ☐   Not yet ☐

   If you answered yes, how do you frame it in the positive?

   _____

   If you answered not yet, the questions that follow could change your perspective.

2. Is it at the Goldilocks level, not too easy and not too hard but just right?

   Yes ☐   Not yet ☐

   If you answered not yet, how can you create the "just right" level of challenge?

   _____

3. Do you have some level of control or choice over your goal?

   Yes ☐   Not yet ☐

   If you answered yes, how did you obtain that control?

   _____

   If you answered not yet, what can you do to assert that control?

   _____

4. Can you connect the behavior to a core value? (We will discuss core values further in activity 19.)

Yes ☐   Not yet ☐

If you answered yes, what is that core value?

_____

If you answered not yet, what core value would you like to tie to your behavior?

_____

5. Can you find a higher purpose for this behavior? (See more about purpose in activity 19.)

Yes ☐   Not yet ☐

If you answered yes, what is that higher purpose?

_____

If you answered not yet, can you imagine a higher purpose for your goal?

_____

At this point, you should have a good understanding of what grit is and how gritty you are right now. You should also have identified a grit goal for yourself.

The next chapters will give you the tools you need to develop both a grittier mind-set (chapter 2) and grittier behavior (chapter 3). By adjusting your thinking (mind-set) and your behavior, you will be on your way to a grittier you!

CHAPTER 2

Developing a Gritty Mind-Set

Change your thoughts and you change your world.

—Norman Vincent Peale

To become grittier, you need to change both the way you think (mind-set) and the way you act (behavior). In this chapter, I will show you ways to develop a *gritty mind-set*. Specifically, I will teach you:

1. To recognize that although you have one brain, you have *two minds*: one that directs you to what feels good in the moment and another that directs you to what will be *beneficial in the long-run*.

2. To identify and challenge common *thinking traps* in order to discover ways of thinking that will support the new, grittier you.

3. To learn how to think in more *optimistic ways* to encourage a *growth mind-set*.

4. To see the power of adding one word to your vocabulary—*yet*.

5. To view failure as an essential step along the path to growth and to learn to see your *mistakes as a learning opportunity*.

Mind-set matters, and by developing your mind-set in this way, you will learn to become more persistent and resilient.

Remember to keep your grit goal in mind as you work through this chapter's activities to develop your gritty mind-set.

6 your two minds: connecting to your future self

You can't build a long term future on short term thinking.

—Billy Cox

for you to know

Often when we are trying to work on our grit goal, there may be two competing voices in our heads: a loud, impulsive voice directing us toward more immediate rewards, and a quiet, thoughtful voice encouraging us to consider long-term outcomes. When you are trying to stick to a goal or overcome a challenge, you will be more successful if you can tune into what you know will feel good in the *long term* and quiet down what feels good *right now* (in the short term). By adopting a mind-set that focuses on the long term, your grit will grow.

We often gravitate to what feels good in the moment because we fall into the *present bias*—that is, a tendency to value immediate rewards at the expense of future goals.[17] We do this because the future can feel abstract and intangible, while the present moment is right in front of us.[18] We feel disconnected from our future self, making it harder to connect with how we might feel when our long-term goal is accomplished. For example, in the moment, we might choose to eat that piece of cake because its deliciousness is crystal clear, whereas our long-term goal about health is less apparent. Our present bias makes short-term attractions more tempting.

In addition, we tend to be overly optimistic about our future self, expecting that in the future we will make better decisions.[19] But when the future comes, we are once again our present-biased selves. For example, maybe you plan to wake up early on Saturday morning to study. But when Saturday comes, you can't get up. So you say to yourself, *I'll get up early next Saturday*, thinking that you'll be more motivated next Saturday.

However, when next week comes—surprise, surprise—you are the same person you were last week: the person who wants to stay in bed. Nothing has changed! This process causes us to favor a reward that arrives sooner rather than later, even if the later reward is better. We choose a few minutes of sleep (small reward) over the good grades that extra studying might bring (big reward).

This is not to say that there is no place for what feels good in the moment. There absolutely is! It's okay to eat the occasional piece of cake, to sleep in, or just let loose. But my goal is for you to be in charge of your brain as opposed to having part of your brain be in charge of you.

for you to do

Here are some examples of short-term and long-term thinking by domain. Use these examples to help you answer the questions that follow.

How Our Two Minds Can Undermine or Promote Grit

Domain	Thinking That Undermines Grit	Thinking That Promotes Grit
Academic	This math problem is too hard. I quit!	This problem is tough, but I will break it down. Also, tough means I'm learning.
Social Relationship	I am not going to the party. There will be no one for me to talk to.	I might know a few people at the party, and if I go, I will get to know them better.
Wellness/Health	I'm not going to the gym. I'm too tired.	Every time I work out, I feel so much better afterward.
Extracurricular	This dance move is too hard. I am done!	No one gets better unless they keep trying, so I will keep practicing.
Emotional	AAAHH!!! [Yelling when someone gets on your nerves.]	Take a deep breath and count to ten. If I yell, then people will only notice how angry I am, and they won't listen to my ideas.

Do you notice that the thinking that *undermines* grit is dominated by a focus on *what feels good in the moment,* whereas thinking that *promotes* grit is dominated by a focus on *what will feel good in the long run*?

Now it's your turn.

Thinking about your own *two minds* and how your thoughts undermine or promote grit, answer the following questions:

How do you think about your grit strength? Do you have a more *long-term* focus?

_____

In the domain where you feel less gritty (your grit goal), do you think more about what feels good in the *short term*?

_____

Did you notice the connection between long-term thinking and more grit?

_____

In contrast, did you notice the connection between short-term thinking and less grit?

_____

If you wanted to share something you have learned in this activity with your Twitter followers, what would you say? You have 140 characters, including spaces.

Example: "be #longterm minded" or #havegritdontquit"

Your tweet: _____

let's dig deeper

Researchers have found that when participants were asked to make choices about future decisions while looking at a digitally aged version of themselves, they were able to think more clearly and concretely about the long term, and their tendency to favor short-term rewards was greatly reduced.[20]

Keeping these findings in mind, imagine yourself *five years from now*. How might you look on Facebook, Instagram, or Snapchat (or whatever we might be using then)? Try to provide lots of details so the image is really clear. Now think about your grit goal and draw a picture of your future self accomplishing this goal, or describe how your future self might feel once your goal has been accomplished.

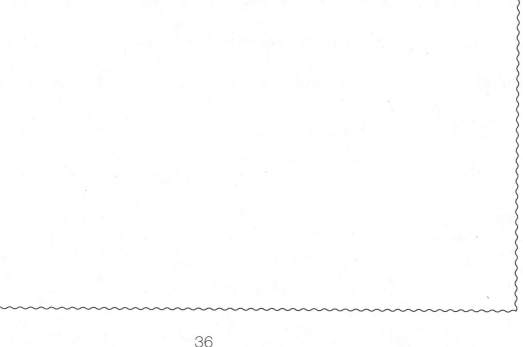

Did picturing your future self help you? Why or why not?

_____

When thinking about your grit goal, see if you can focus on the *long term* as opposed to the short term. Ask yourself: *In the future, what will really be important to me?* When we are able to imagine and connect to a vision of our future selves, we are more likely to be gritty and persevere.

In the next activity, you will learn how to uncover the thinking traps that might be sabotaging your success. You will learn to quiet thinking that is getting in your way (short-term thinking) and strengthen thinking (long-term/future thinking) that supports a grittier you.

7 uncovering your thinking traps

There is nothing either good or bad but thinking makes it so.

—William Shakespeare

for you to know

Your mind-set, or the way you choose to think about things, is very powerful. Remember Lisa in activity 3? She was strong in her academic grit, but her social grit was weaker, partly because she was *thinking* about each domain with her two different minds. Lisa viewed academic challenges as learning opportunities and steps toward her long-term goal of going to college. But when she faced a social challenge, she was more likely to think, *I will always feel awkward and uncomfortable, so I might as well just stay home.* Her mind-set kept the costs of social encounters—the stress of striking up conversations, the potential for embarrassment—front and center. In terms of her social grit, Lisa was falling into *common thinking traps,* or what psychologist Albert Ellis calls "irrational thoughts." Irrational thoughts or thinking traps were preventing Lisa from reaching her goal.

Common thinking traps include:

- *Demandingness—Shoulds/Musts!* The belief that things and conditions absolutely must be the way you want them to be. This belief often features words like should, must, have to, need, and ought. For example, *This should not be so hard!* or, *My friends should not be acting that way.*

- *Awfulizing—It Is Terrible!* The belief that situations and/or events are awful, terrible, or catastrophic. For example, *Making a mistake is the worst thing ever!* or *I will never be able to finish this chapter!*

- *Low Frustration Tolerance—I Can't Stand It!* The belief that struggle is unbearable and must be avoided at all costs. For example, *If no one talks to me at the party, I will just die!*

- *Global Rating of Self/Others; Self-Downing.* The belief that we can be defined by one negative aspect. For example, *If I get a bad grade on my social studies test, there is something wrong with me.*[21]

Do any of these thinking traps sound familiar? When you find yourself falling into a thinking trap, ask yourself:

- What is the evidence that what I'm thinking is true?

- How is this thinking helpful?

- What would I say to a friend who was thinking this way?

This may lead you to realize that your irrational thoughts are not true, not helpful, and not the way you would advise a good friend who is in the same situation.

Now, instead, let's develop rational ways of thinking that can help you think grittier as you work toward a long-term goal:

- *Wishes/ Preferences:* A wish or preference is softer and more flexible than a *should*. It can be the desire to have things the way you would like without demanding that it must be so. For example, *I wish this wasn't so hard for me, but "shoulding" on myself doesn't solve anything.*

- *Living in the Gray:* The belief that while an event might be inconvenient, it is not awful. For example, *Although no one likes to get a bad grade, it's not the worst thing that could happen.*

- *High Frustration Tolerance/ I Can Stand It:* The belief that while we may dislike something, we can *actually* stand it. For example, *I may not like it, but I can stand it!*

- *Unconditional Self-Acceptance:* The belief that we are more than just one negative aspect of ourselves. For example, *I messed up on that science test, but I am not a worthless human being.*

for you to do

Keeping your grit goal in mind:

1. Think about a time when you fell into a thinking trap. Write down a sentence that reflects your irrational thoughts. For example, *Writing is so hard, I just can't stand it.*

   _____

2. Circle the thinking trap(s) you used.

   Demandingness—Shoulds/Musts

   Awfulizing—It Is Terrible!

   Low Frustration Tolerance—I Can't Stand It!

   Global Rating of Self/Others; Self-Downing

3. Now try to challenge those thinking traps by asking yourself:

   What is the evidence that what I am thinking is true?

   How is this thinking helpful?

   What would I say to a friend who was thinking this way?

4. See if you can come up with a way of thinking that is both rational and helpful. For example, *I wish writing wasn't so hard for me, but I can stand it.*

   _____

   _____

5. Circle the rational/helpful thoughts you used.

     Wishes/ Preferences

     Living in the Gray

     High Frustration Tolerance/ I Can Stand It

     Unconditional Self-Acceptance

6. When you used rational thinking to address your grit goal, did you feel more inspired and more likely to persevere?

Yes ☐   *Not yet* ☐

let's dig deeper

You have been relying on your irrational thoughts/thinking traps for a while, so don't be discouraged if it takes time for this new way of thinking to take hold. Just keep practicing your new rational thoughts; eventually they'll become your way of thinking!

Over the next week, log your irrational thoughts/thinking traps as they relate to your grit goal. Then challenge them as I've shown you and replace them with rational thoughts. Before you begin, look at this completed example:

Grit Goal: Academic Grit

Day of the Week	Event	Irrational Thoughts	Challenges	Rational Thoughts
Monday	Teacher gave me five pages of challenging math problems.	*School is too hard! I can't stand it! I'm not doing it!*	What is the evidence? How is this helpful? Would I say this to a friend?	*Although school is hard, I can stand it. I have done it before. Saying school is hard is not helpful. It just discourages me more.*

Now you try. (If you need more space, you can download the worksheet at http://www.newharbinger.com/38563.)

Grit Goal: _____

Day of the Week	Event	Irrational Thoughts	Challenges	Rational Thoughts
Monday				
Tuesday				
Wednesday				
Thursday				
Friday				
Saturday				
Sunday				

Now that you have learned about common thinking traps, in the next activity we'll look at a specific thinking trap that undermines grit: pessimism.

8 goodbye pessimism, hello optimism

A pessimist sees the difficulty in every opportunity;
an optimist sees the opportunity in every difficulty.

—Winston Churchill

for you to know

Pessimism is the tendency to see the worst aspect of things or believe that the worst will happen. It is a lack of hope or confidence in the future. Let's see how you can turn pessimism around by cultivating optimism.

Say you're working to improve your emotional grit. You have anxiety about being able to sleep away from home, and you challenge yourself to face this by going on the senior class overnight trip. Initially, you might think, *I can't go on this trip. It's going to be awful. I will never fall asleep, and I'm going to miss everything I'm used to from home.* Or you might think, *It's important for me to go on this trip because I am going to college soon and I have to learn to sleep in a new environment. If I can't fall asleep, then I won't fall asleep. I'll be tired, but I will survive.* Both ways of thinking are based on the same situation—the senior class overnight trip. But the first way is pessimistic, expecting the worst and pick, pick, picking out all the potential problems, while the second way is optimistic, focusing on the positive aspects of the trip and why the trip is important in the long run.

Research shows that having an *optimistic mind-set* is linked to grit. When you are optimistic you are more likely to persevere when faced with a challenge. Furthermore, people who are more optimistic rate themselves as happier, which in turn predicts grit and overall success.[22] Although some people are just naturally more optimistic or pessimistic than others, you *can* learn to be more optimistic.[23]

Let's see what we can learn by examining how optimists and pessimists think.

How Do Optimists Think?

Optimists are more likely to think of the bad things that happen to them as temporary and specific events set against a backdrop of mostly good. For example, an optimistic person might consider a bad grade on a test as just one bad grade among many. When we tell ourselves that we failed because of something temporary and specific, we are more likely to keep trying.

My Mother, an Example of an Optimist

My mother always sees the good in every situation. Once, when she was babysitting my kids, she got locked out of the house. It was getting dark, but my mother made it an "adventure" by turning the search for the keys into a scavenger hunt under the stars. Another time, when we were hiking together in Arizona, my mother brushed up against a cactus and got lots of painful needles stuck in her arm and leg. At first she cried out in pain, but shortly afterward she said, "When we look back at this, it will make a good story."

Think about a challenge you've had. Did it wind up making a good story?

How Do Pessimists Think?

People with a pessimistic attitude think that failure is terrible and personal and will happen again. A pessimistic person with a bad test grade thinks, *I'm terrible at chemistry and I always will be*, and is reluctant to try again. Pessimistic people fall into what Martin Seligman, the founder of positive psychology, has called the *Problematic P's*:

- Permanence—Pessimists believe that bad events are permanent and persistent—that is, they will never change.

- Pervasiveness—Pessimists believe that bad events are universal and pervasive—that is, they are everywhere.

- Personalization—Pessimists believe that bad events reflect on them personally and not the situation—that is, "It's all about *me*."[24]

Optimists	Pessimists
I didn't get a great grade on this math test, but that doesn't mean I will do poorly the next time. (Temporary)	*I did badly on this math test, which means I will do badly on every math test.* (Permanent)
I had a poor at-bat in today's baseball game, but each hit is unrelated to the others. If I practice, I bet I can do better next time. (Specific)	*Hitting poorly makes me a terrible pitcher, hitter, catcher, overall player, and human being.* (Pervasive)
Sophia passed me in the hall and didn't say hello. She must be having a bad day. (Situational)	*Sophia passed me in the hall and didn't say hello. She must hate me.* (Personal)

for you to do

1. Do you consider yourself more of an optimist or a pessimist? Circle your answer.

   Optimist   Pessimist

2. When bad things happen, do you ever fall into the Problematic P's? If you do, circle your most common problematic P:

   Making It Permanent   Making It Pervasive   Taking It Personally

3. Think about a recent setback or challenge you faced when you engaged in pessimistic thinking? If you had a thought bubble over your head (like a cartoon character), what would be in the bubble?

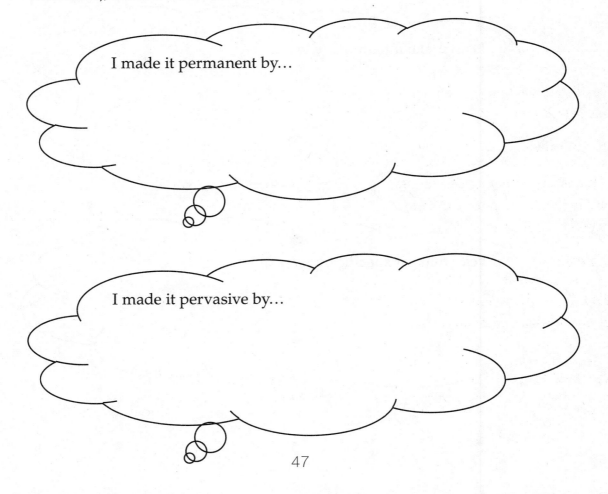

I made it permanent by…

I made it pervasive by…

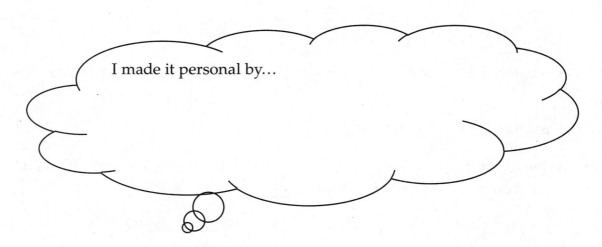

I made it personal by…

Thinking about that same setback or challenge, can you engage in more optimistic thinking? What would be in your thought bubble now?

I can make it temporary by…

I can make it specific by…

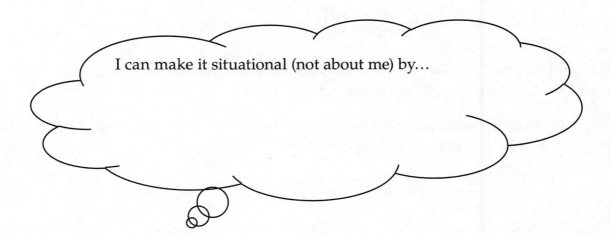

I can make it situational (not about me) by...

let's dig deeper

Every time something happens that can be perceived as bad, try to find the good. Or, as my mother would say, "Turn it into an adventure."

Think about a challenge you have faced in striving to meet your grit goal. How might you turn it around and see it in a more optimistic light?

_____

_____

When you see the good, how do you feel?

_____

Does seeing the good inspire you?

_____

Can you think about how, in the future, the challenge you faced will make a really good story?

_____

When growing your grit, try to turn your _Problematic P's_ (permanent, pervasive, and personal) into _Promoting P's_ (passion, perseverance, and purpose)!

In the next activity, you will learn how to develop a _growth mind-set_ to make even more progress toward your grit goal.

nurturing a growth mind-set 9

Becoming is better than being.

—Carol S. Dweck

for you to know

Did you know that your talent, intelligence, and abilities can *change* through hard work, use of effective strategies, and help from others? This message is at the heart of psychologist Carol Dweck's research on developing a growth mind-set.[25] Those with a growth mind-set believe that their brain and abilities can grow with effort. When learning or doing something new and challenging—be it an instrument, a dance move, or facing fears—they understand that hard work can help them accomplish their goals. They might say, "I may not know how to do this *now*, but with effort and hard work, I can learn." People with a growth mind-set also believe that they can learn from challenges and setbacks. Research suggests that having a growth mind-set is one of the keys to building grit.[26]

A fixed mind-set is the opposite of a growth mind-set. Someone with a fixed mind-set believes that his abilities and brain are "fixed." He might say, "I'm bad at math, so there is no point in studying." A person with a fixed mind-set believes that either she is smart or talented or she's not. I often hear teens say "If you need to study for a subject, you're not that smart." Or, after just one attempt, someone with a fixed mind-set would say, "I'm terrible at water-skiing," rather than thinking *Why would I be good at it? I've only done it once*! If you have a fixed mind-set, you are likely to interpret any setback as evidence that you don't have what it takes—and quit. Having a fixed mind-set reduces your motivation and makes it harder to complete long-term goals.

In reality, we all have some areas where we display more of a fixed mind-set and some where we display more of a growth mind-set. Dweck has identified five areas where people tend to vary in their mind-set: *effort, obstacles, challenges, criticism,* and *success of others.*[27] Just as you may vary in your level of grit by domains, you may vary by area in your ability to maintain a growth mind-set.

A Person with a Growth Mind-set	A Person with a Fixed Mind-set
Believes that *effort* is the way to get smarter and that intelligence can be developed through learning. *The way you get smarter is by working wisely.*	Views *effort* negatively. Believes intelligence is a fixed trait. *If you're smart, you don't have to work. Either you're smart or you're not.*
Perseveres when faced with an *obstacle*. *I messed up during my tennis match, but if I work with a coach, I will improve.*	Gives up when faced with an *obstacle* or setback. *I messed up during my tennis match, so I should quit.*
Seeks *challenging* work because that is where learning takes place. *Taking honors classes will be more work, but I will learn more.*	Seeks easy, *unchallenging* work. *If I take easy classes, I can get an easy A.*
Views asking for help, *criticism*, or negative feedback as aiding learning. *I ask for help when I am stuck. Asking for help is the way to get better. If I get feedback, my skills can grow.*	Ignores *criticism*, no matter how constructive. Is reluctant to ask for help. *If I ask for help, my teachers will think I am stupid.*
Sees other people's *success* as inspirational and educational. *I want to surround myself with successful, high-achieving students and learn from them.*	Views other people's *success* as a threat. Wants to appear smart. *I don't want to take a challenging class or take on a tough problem because I need to always look smart.*

Interestingly, learning about the value of a growth mind-set (what you are doing now) changes your belief systems and, ultimately, your level of grit! So you are nurturing a growth mind-set right now. Way to go!

for you to do

It is important to know the areas and conditions in which you display a fixed mind-set (your triggers) and your plan for them. It can be helpful to talk to your inner fixed mind-set when it shows up; maybe even give it a name. See if you can use it to your advantage instead of letting it undermine you.[28]

Write a letter to yourself, showing how you can use a growth mind-set to work toward your grit goal. If your fixed mind-set tries to gain control, recognize it, call it out (give it a name), and use it to help your growth. Read this example:

Dear Caren,

When you find yourself struggling to make healthy choices, try to learn and grow from your mistakes. If you can't do twenty pushups, keep working, because by sticking with it, you will get healthier and stronger. If you eat too many cookies at night, recognize that behavior without putting yourself down (no judgment), and decide you will do something different next time (like stay out of the kitchen after 9 p.m.). You know it is easy for your fixed mind-set to emerge—the part of you that believes you will never change. However, call him out ("Mr. Fixie") and tell him to take a hike. Then give yourself credit for getting back on track. Remember that when you struggle, you are getting stronger, wiser, and better as a result.

Now *you* try.

_____

_____

_____

_____

_____

_____

Change takes time. In the next activity, I will show you the power of *yet*—a way to recognize that the things you want to change about yourself take time—and although you may not be there just *yet*, you are on your way!

The genius is he who sees what is not yet and causes it to come to be.

—Peter Nivio Zarlenga

for you to know

Part of developing a growth mind-set is acknowledging that you are a work in progress and that you will improve with time and effort. That is where the power of yet comes in. By adding the word *yet* to our vocabulary, a concept created by Carol Dweck,[29] we can increase our grit.

For example, if you are not able to play a challenging musical piece (extracurricular domain), solve a difficult math problem (academic domain), or stop yelling at your younger brother (emotional domain), adding the word *yet* to those statements opens up a world of possibilities!

I can't play that challenging musical piece… yet.

I can't solve that math problem… yet.

I can't stop yelling at my younger brother… yet.

By simply adding *yet* to your thinking, you are encouraging optimism, a growth mind-set, and a belief in your ability to change for the positive. This mind-set will allow you to persevere and bounce back from setbacks you might encounter as we move into chapter 3, on promoting gritty behavior. You will be able to see your mistakes as a "first attempt in learning" (F.A.I.L.) (a term coined by former Indian president A.P.J. Abdul Kalam), rather than an end point.

Who would have thought that three letters—Y, E, T—could be so powerful?

But getting to *yet* is not easy. If you are faced with a challenge, a tough situation, or a setback, it is sometime easier to just say "I can't."

So how can you get to *yet*?

1. Take a deep breath. This will help you think more clearly and activate your more thoughtful, mindful, future-oriented self.

2. Focus on your long-term goals rather than on what feels good in the moment—which might be quitting. What you focus on expands in your mind, and what you disregard fades into the background (more about this in activity 15).

3. Try to view challenges as part of the process, not as a reason to stop.

4. Ask for help and get support from family and friends. Social support provides the extra cushion you need to get the hard work done.

Let's Hear from Some Teens

"I get anxious about going to school after a weekend or vacation. Then I get mad at myself for being anxious and, no matter what I do, I can't stop the feeling. However, when I take a deep breath and add one word to my feelings—yet—I feel better. I can't stop the feeling of anxiety—yet. But I will! And in a few minutes, I can get out of bed and face the day."

—Christina, high school freshman

"At hockey practice, we need to do sprints for ten minutes. When the coach yells out, 'Start,' I often say, 'I can't do this.' However, by simply adding the word yet at the end of the sentence, 'I can't do sprints for ten minutes straight yet,' I feel more inspired and am more likely to complete them."

—Andre, high school senior

for you to do

Think about your grit goal and add *yet* to the end of an "I am not/I can't" statement.

For example, if your grit goal is to improve your wellness and health, the exercise might look like this:

1. I can't find time to work out *yet*.

2. I can't do fifteen pushups without stopping *yet*.

3. I can't stop snacking *yet*.

4. I can't stop watching TV when I should be sleeping *yet*.

5. I can't make healthy meal choices *yet*.

Now you try, with your grit goal in mind.

1. _____

2. _____

3. _____

4. _____

5. _____

(Hang onto these *yets*. In activity 13, you will use them to make your SMART goals.)

let's dig deeper

Did adding the word *yet* make you feel more optimistic and more willing to continue working on your grit goal?

Commit to using the word *yet* when talking about challenges. Share the concept of *yet* with your friends and family, and watch your grit soar!

No matter what you set out to do, it is inevitable that you will face failure at some point in the process. In the next activity, you will learn how to embrace failure and see it as just another step on the path (another *yet*) to becoming grittier!

seeing failure as an opportunity for growth 11

for you to know

Even people who are now considered legends once had to overcome failure. For example, Albert Einstein was told he would "never amount to anything," Michael Jordan was cut from his high school basketball team, and Oprah Winfrey was fired from her job as a television reporter because she was "unfit for TV." After feeling the sting of their mistakes and failures, they learned from them. They had to recognize that, in the words of John Lennon, "Everything will be okay in the end, and if it is not okay, it is not yet the end."

Successful people understand that mistakes have value and are part of the process. When you are able to *embrace failure* ("fail forward"), and *learn from it*, it is easier to remain steadfast and open to challenges—in other words, to be grittier.[30]

Ted's Story

Ted is thirteen. He has played goalie in soccer since he was five. Although Ted is a strong player, he gets upset when the other team scores a goal. He feels that he has let his team down and that the game is ruined.

Ted lets his failures on the soccer field define how he feels about himself and the game. If he could find a way to embrace his failures instead of letting them knock him down, he could be grittier—and even improve his game.

What if, when the other team scored, Ted told himself this instead? *When you play goalie, the other team will score. It is just part of the game. I will not get mad at myself for what is a natural part of the game (and life). My team knows I am trying my best. And I know I am trying my best. The next time I am at practice, I will work with my coach to get better at covering all corners of the goal.*

With this way of thinking, do you think Ted will be more successful?

Do you think Ted will feel better?

Do you think Ted will grow as a soccer player?

Emma's Story

Emma never felt like she belonged in high school and was very excited about getting a fresh start in college. But during freshman orientation, she had a hard time connecting with people. When the other students asked her name, she could not even say it right; it came out, "E-E-Emma." She felt stupid and believed that, once again, she would not have any friends. When she got home, she told her parents she hated school.

How could Emma reframe her experience?

She might think, *I bet lots of people felt nervous at freshman orientation. Just because I had a hard time once, that doesn't mean I will next time. If I just keep putting myself out there, I will get better at being more social and make a friend.*

By changing her thinking, do you think Emma will be more likely to persist at her goal of connecting with people?

Do you think she will be more successful? Will she feel better?

Do you think Emma will ultimately get better at introducing herself in social situations?

for you to do

Keeping your grit goal in mind, answer these questions.

1. Think about a time when you experienced a failure or made a mistake. Describe it here.

   _____

   _____

2. What was your initial reaction when you first experienced the failure or made the mistake? Did you fall into any of the Problematic P's from activity 8?

   _____

3. How did you feel when you didn't accomplish what you set out to do? Write about the feeling. (Remember, it often hurts when we fail, but don't let the feeling crush you. Instead, use it to energize your next effort.)

   _____

4. Use that feeling of disappointment as a *cue* to change the way you think. Try instead to (a) keep it small (not catastrophize/not make it *pervasive*), (b) take in the whole situation (don't *personalize*), (c) stay in the present moment (don't generalize or make it *permanent*), and (d) learn from it (grow). Now write about your challenge using your new perspective.

   _____

   _____

5. Did this new perspective make you feel better and more willing to persevere?

   Yes ☐   *Not yet* ☐

let's dig deeper

When it comes to dealing with challenging situations, are you a carrot, an egg, or instant cocoa?

What do I mean? Well, think about how each of these responds when placed in hot water. A carrot gets *soft*, an egg *hardens,* and cocoa gets *better.* The next time you face a challenge (get in hot water), especially as it relates to your grit goal, see if you can be more like cocoa and get *better*!

If you didn't answer cocoa, could you be more like cocoa the next time you are in hot water? What mind-set strategies discussed in this chapter can you use?

_____

_____

_____

_____

_____

let's review our gritty mind-set 12

In order to succeed, we must first believe that we can.

—Nikos Kazantzakis

In this chapter, you have learned strategies to help you develop a gritty mind-set—the first step in strengthening your grit. In the next chapter, you will learn about gritty behavior and how you can put your thoughts into action.

First let's see how well you have understood key gritty mind-set concepts. Keeping your grit goal in mind:

1. Can you activate the part of your mind that focuses on your long-term, future self?

   Yes ☐　　*Not yet* ☐

2. Did you discover the thinking traps that are undermining your grit?

   Yes ☐　　*Not yet* ☐

3. Have you started to develop new, more rational ways of thinking?

   Yes ☐　　*Not yet* ☐

4. Do you feel more optimistic and less likely to fall into the Problematic P's?

   Yes ☐　　*Not yet* ☐

5. Do you see the benefits of a growth mind-set?

   Yes ☐　　*Not yet* ☐

6. Have you seen the power of *yet*?

   Yes ☐　　*Not yet* ☐

7. Can you see mistakes as your friend and failure as an opportunity for growth?

   Yes ☐　　*Not yet* ☐

Now let's put those thoughts into action and learn about gritty behavior!

CHAPTER 3

Developing Gritty Behavior

It isn't what we say or think that defines us, but what we do.

—Andrew Davies

As you know, to be gritty you need both motivation (mind-set) and volition (behavior)—the *formula* for grit. While being motivated to be gritty is important, if motivation is not accompanied by a change in behavior, you will not get the results you want. For example, it's not enough to be motivated to be a great guitar player; you need to *pick up the instrument and practice*! It is not enough to think how great you would feel if you were less worried; you need to behave in ways that lessen your anxiety.

In this chapter, I will show you how to:

1. Set and commit to *effective goals* that are specific, manageable, and important to you.

2. Practice the steps needed to achieve your goals, using *deliberate practice*.

3. Keep your goals *front and center* so they are always directing you.

4. *Practice self-control.* Working toward your goals is not easy; it takes self-control to behave in ways that are gritty.

5. Turn your new behavior into a *habit* so it becomes automatic.

The techniques are based on the latest research as well as tips from teens like *you*!

As you work through the activities in this chapter to develop gritty behavior, always keep your grit goal in mind.

13 setting effective goals

A dream is just a dream. A goal is a dream with a plan and a deadline.

—Harvey MacKay

for you to know

Setting effective goals is an essential first step to achieving gritty behavior because each goal met brings you one step closer to transforming your gritty mind-set from dream to reality. In this activity, you will learn how to break your grit goal into smaller, more specific components—called *SMART goals*, the building blocks of your larger grit goal.[31]

SMART stands for:

S—Specific (or Significant)

M—Measurable (or Meaningful)

A—Attainable (or Action-Oriented)

R—Relevant (or Rewarding)

T—Time-Bound (or Trackable)

Let's say your grit goal is to be socially grittier. You have the motivation (being socially grittier is important to you), and you have adjusted your mind-set (you are embracing optimism and trying to adopt a growth mind-set). These are great first steps, but alone they aren't enough. The next—and crucial—step is to set a SMART goal, or goals, that will lead you toward a greater change. For example, you might set yourself the following SMART goal: *The next time I am at lunch, I will wave at someone I know from one of my classes.* Setting smaller goals within the domain you have selected is one way to turn your gritty mind-set into action.

More about SMART goals:

SMART goals are *specific*; they state as clearly as possible what it is you'll do and when (*I will go to the gym on Monday at 10 a.m. to take a kickboxing class*).

SMART goals are also *measurable*; you can easily see whether you've achieved the goal (*I will talk to one person at lunch today*).

SMART goals are *attainable*. It's not something you *won't* do—*I won't spend time online when I should be studying*—which is just a hope. It's something you *can* and *will* do.

SMART goals are directly *relevant* to your target—progress in the domain you're working to get grittier in—and they're *rewarding*. When you make it to kickboxing class, for example, you'll get the satisfaction of knowing you're getting that much grittier with your wellness.

SMART goals are *time-bound* and *trackable*. You set them with a clear time frame for completing them. And you give yourself ways to track your progress: for example, checking off on your calendar each time you made it to kickboxing class. Or, telling a friend about your commitment, and having that friend check in to see if you're keeping up with it and noting when you're not.

In sum, SMART goals give you structure, clarity, motivation, and accountability. That makes them great goals to set when you're just starting to get gritty in a certain area.

Let's try setting a few now.

for you to do

For the following activity, focus on your grit goal.

Within this domain, think of one SMART goal. First review these examples.

SMART Goal	Social/Relationship Domain	Academic Domain
S—Specific (or Significant)	*I will talk to one new person during college orientation.*	*I will record my homework assignments in the notes section of my phone.*
M—Measurable (or Meaningful)	*This is meaningful because I want to make friends in college. If I talk to one new person, it will help me overcome my fear.*	*This is meaningful because I can't forget to do my homework. I will record (measure) my homework assignment in the calendar of my phone.*
A—Attainable (or Action-Oriented)	*This is attainable because it is just one person.*	*This is attainable because I always have my phone.*
R—Relevant (or Rewarding)	*I'm doing this for the reward of being more connected with others.*	*This is relevant because I hate scrambling and feeling unprepared.*
T—Time-Bound (or Trackable)	*I will do this during the first hour of college orientation.*	*I will set a reminder for myself each day and will show my phone to a friend or family member at the end of the week.*

Now try making a SMART goal for yourself.

SMART Goal	Domain: _____
S—Specific (or Significant)	
M—Measurable (or Meaningful)	
A—Attainable (or Action-Oriented)	
R—Relevant (or Rewarding)	
T—Time-Bound (or Trackable)	

Since SMART goals should be small and achievable, you will need to continue setting more goals to truly grow your gritty behavior. However, start small, and let success breed success.

let's dig deeper

Now that you have learned how to make a SMART goal, try making four more (for a total of five) that fit under your grit goal umbrella.

One way to develop your SMART goals is to review the list of things to which you have added *yet* back in activity 10. For example, see how I turned my *yets* from activity 10 into SMART goals.

Yets	SMART Goals
1. I can't find the time to work out, yet.	1. I will work out on Tuesday and Friday mornings.
2. I can't do 15 pushups without stopping, yet.	2. I will do ten pushups when I wake up in the morning and five more before I go to bed.
3. I can't stop snacking at night, yet.	3. I will stay out of the kitchen after 9 p.m.
4. I can't stop watching TV when I should be sleeping, yet.	4. I will go to bed at 11 p.m. during the week.
5. I can't make healthy meal choices, yet.	5. I will eat an egg or oatmeal for breakfast every day.

Now you try.

Yets	SMART Goals
1.	1.
2.	2.
3.	3.
4.	4.
5.	5.

Practice these SMART goals over the next few weeks. I encourage you to place written goal reminders where you will see them every day—say, taped to your bathroom mirror, or set daily reminders in your phone. Writing really helps turn your gritty mind-set into gritty behavior.

Also, let people know about your goal(s) so that you can receive support along the way. By *sharing* your goals and making them public, you will feel more motivated to complete them.

If there's a day you don't meet a particular goal, don't put yourself down. Just try your best to *learn from* your stumble—which may involve trying different strategies and/or tweaking a goal slightly.

As you work on these goals, be sure to acknowledge and savor all your wins, no matter how small.[32] For example, if you are trying to get to the gym more often, give yourself credit even if you get through only half a class. You can also give yourself small *rewards*.

Now write down a few rewards you can give yourself for making and working on each of your SMART goals:

_____

_____

_____

practicing makes perfect 14

Genius is one percent inspiration and ninety-nine percent perspiration.

—Thomas A. Edison

for you to know

You may have noticed that some of your SMART goals were easy to accomplish, but some gave you more trouble. When I was trying to lose weight, for example, I found it easy to go to the gym and eat a healthy breakfast, but not engaging in late night snacking was tough! For me, resisting the urge to snack at night brought out the part of my mind that focuses on what feels good in the moment. To reach those tough goals or to target a weakness, you need *deliberate practice*.

What is deliberate practice? It is a particular type of strategy that gritty people use to improve performance and achieve their goals: focused, intentional practice combined with feedback from experts (a teacher or coach) and lots of repetition. [33] Think of a baseball player practicing her swing repeatedly or a musician playing the same tricky section of a music score again and again.

Deliberate practice is a little different from the SMART goals you made in the previous activity. The goals you will be striving for in this activity using deliberate practice will *stretch you*. This means they will take a little more time. They are the goals you might shy away from or put at the end of your to-do list. Deliberate practice isn't always fun, but it is an investment in improving yourself.[34]

Formula for Deliberate Practice:

1. Identify your weakness or weaknesses.

2. Set a specific stretch goal.

3. Practice for as long as you can concentrate and set a consistent schedule for this practice.

4. Make a mental representation for yourself of what you want to accomplish. (You may know this technique as *visualization*).

5. Seek out and receive regular feedback from a coach or mentor.

6. Stay focused (no multitasking).

7. Work at the edge of your abilities (outside your comfort zone).

8. Work on your area of weakness until it is mastered.

for you to do

Kenton's Story

Kenton is the captain of his tennis team, regularly wins tournaments, and gets a lot of praise for his tennis playing. He practices before and after school and works with his coach to perfect the parts of his game that need improvement. While Kenton has a strong forehand and backhand, his toss for his serve is weak. To address this, before starting his toss, Kenton visualizes and creates a mental representation of how it should look: high, straight, and consistent. He works on his toss for fifteen minutes (the amount of time he can concentrate fully) and always at the beginning of his practice session. During practice, he gets feedback from his coach, which he takes into account when he practices on his own. Sometimes Kenton is tempted to practice his forehands and backhands, but he forces himself to stay focused on his toss. All of this practice can be tedious, but Kenton sticks with it because he knows his hard work will pay off.

What aspects of deliberate practice were mentioned in Kenton's story?

Has Kenton...

1. Identified a specific area of weakness? What is it?

    _____

2. Set a specific stretch goal? What is it?

    _____

3. Practiced for as long as he could concentrate and set a consistent schedule for this practice?

    Yes ☐   *Not yet* ☐

4. Created a mental representation or image of his goal?

    Yes ☐   *Not yet* ☐

5. Sought out and received regular feedback from an expert?

    Yes ☐   *Not yet* ☐

6. Remained focused?

    Yes ☐   *Not yet* ☐

7. Worked at the edge of his abilities?

    Yes ☐   *Not yet* ☐

8. Worked on his area of weakness until it is mastered?

    Yes ☐   *Not yet* ☐

let's dig deeper

See if you can apply deliberate practice to a SMART goal that is giving you trouble.

Have you...

1. Identified your weakness that you will apply deliberate practice to?

   _____

2. Set a specific stretch goal? What is it?

   _____

3. Practiced for as long as you could concentrate and set a consistent schedule for this practice?

   Yes ☐   Not yet ☐

4. Made a mental representation of your goal?

   Yes ☐   Not yet ☐

5. Sought out feedback from an expert? (Sometimes it is hard to show your weakness to others, but that is what you need to do in order to improve.)

   Yes ☐   Not yet ☐

6. Who can you receive feedback from? _____

7. Remained focused on your weakness? (Remember, no multitasking.)

   Yes ☐   Not yet ☐

8. Worked at your edge? You should feel the tension, but not so much that it is unbearable.

   Yes ☐   Not yet ☐

9. Worked on your weakness until it is mastered? How will you do that?

_____

Deliberate practice is an essential step you need to turn your grit goal into a reality.

putting what you want to achieve front and center 15

The eye sees all, but the mind shows us what we want to see.

—William Shakespeare

for you to know

Having goals and using deliberate practice are both important to increasing your gritty behavior. However, you need to keep these goals *front and center* so you are never tempted to stray. In this activity, you will learn just that—to shine a light on your goals so they are always visible to you.

Try this simple experiment to see how important it is to make your goals the center of your attention.

Look around your current surroundings and try to find all the *red* things that you can see. Give yourself twenty seconds to look around.

Okay, so what did you see that was *green*?

You may be thinking, *Green? I thought you said red!*

I did, but you looked around, right? So why couldn't you tell me what was green?[35]

The reason is that what we focus on (the red) expands in our mind while everything else (in this case, the green) fades away.

What does this have to do with *goal setting* and *highlighting our goals*? When we keep our focus on our goals and what we want to accomplish in the long run, these come to the forefront and become prominent in our lives.

Making Advantage Cards

One way to do this is by making an Advantage Card, a technique developed by psychologist Judith Beck.[36] The idea is to put the advantages for your new gritty behavior in writing and to read them each day you can. Use them for any grit goal you have. Advantage Cards help you persist even when the going gets tough. As you will recall from activity 6, when we make our goals more concrete and tangible—which Advantage Cards do—we can maintain more long-term thinking and gritty behavior.

Examples of Advantage Cards

The Advantages of Being Grittier Academically	The Advantages of Being Grittier Emotionally (Less Anxious)
I will feel better in class when I am prepared. I have a better chance of making the honor roll. I will have more options open to me when I finish school and graduate. I will be acting more responsibly, something that is important to me to do. My parents and teachers will stop nagging me.	I will be happier. I will be able to do the things I like. I will feel more confident at school. I will have more fun. I will feel proud that I accomplished something that is challenging for me.

for you to do

Now you try. Make an Advantage Card for your grit goal. (If you like, you can download blank Advantage Cards at http://www.newharbinger.com/38563.)

The Advantages of Being Grittier

_____

---

let's dig deeper

Once you have written your Advantage card, decide where and when you will look at it. Many people choose to leave the card on their nightstand or in the bathroom so they can read it first thing in the morning or before going to bed.

When will you read your Advantage Card? _____ (time)

Where will you keep it? _____ (place)

Setting goals and keeping them visible are important steps to increasing gritty behavior. However, this endeavor takes *work,* and there are many temptations along the way. In the next activity, we will examine how self-control contributes to gritty behavior.

developing self-control: how 16
to not eat the marshmallow

The most important scientific discovery about self-control is that it can be taught.

—Walter Mischel

for you to know

In the late 1960s and early 1970s, psychologist Walter Mischel conducted research that became famous as the "marshmallow experiment." He left four-year-olds alone in a room with no distractions and one delicious marshmallow. The children were told that they could have either one marshmallow now or, if they could wait, two marshmallows later.

Videos of the children left alone in the room with the marshmallow showed that those who were able to wait exhibited the following behavior (or explained their internal coping later):

- They did not look at the marshmallow, they walked away from the marshmallow, or they distracted themselves by singing or playing with their hands or feet.

- They imagined the marshmallow as something abstract, like a cloud or a picture of a marshmallow.

- They imagined that the marshmallow was something undesirable.

- They kept their focus on the end goal (two marshmallows instead of one).

In contrast, those children who could not wait were seen (or later reported):

- Staring at and/or holding the marshmallow.

- Smelling the marshmallow.

- Thinking how yummy it would be to eat it.

Dr. Mischel followed these children as they grew up and discovered that the children who were able to wait—who exhibited greater self-control—went on to have better outcomes later in life, like higher SAT scores, exceptional educational achievement, greater self-esteem, and more capacity to cope with stress.[37]

Although you may not have to choose between one marshmallow now or two later, you will need to choose between checking Instagram now or studying for a test, between sleeping in or getting up early for swim practice—in other words, between long-term goals and short-term "rewards" (or what feel like rewards in the moment).

(It is important to note that while self-control and grit go hand in hand, they are distinct. Self-control means delaying gratification and resisting temptations *in the moment,* while grit is the ability to persevere and remain on track *over the long term.* But gritty people know that real results materialize only when they are able to resist instant gratification. So by practicing self-control, you will be able to grow your grit.)[38]

Strategies for Self-Control

What can we learn from the preschoolers who were able to resist that marshmallow? That it is better to *avoid temptation and change the way you think about the temptation* as opposed to *relying on sheer willpower.*

Here is a list of five research-based scientific strategies for self-control.[39] They are listed in order of effectiveness, meaning it is better to use an earlier rather than a later strategy. This part is a little technical, but stick with me.

1. *Situation Selection*: The best strategy for self-control is to put yourself in situations or settings that favor your long-term goals and avoid places where you will be

tempted. For example, if you know that it will be hard to accomplish your wellness goal by going to a party where there will be drinking, don't go. (The preschoolers didn't have this option: they were in the room with the marshmallow.)

2. *Situation Modification*: Sometimes you can't avoid temptation altogether, but you can change a situation to your advantage. If, for example, you want to study more but you find the Internet distracting, turn off the Wi-Fi or use an app that disconnects you from the Internet. (This is what the preschoolers did when they walked away from the marshmallow.)

3. *Selective Attention*: If you are unable to avoid or change a situation, focus your attention in a way that will help you resist temptation, rather than undermine self-control. For example, if you are working on a wellness goal of eating fewer sweets, skip the dessert section in the school cafeteria. (This is what the preschoolers did when they looked away from the marshmallow.)

4. *Cognitive Change*: Reframe the temptation. For example, instead of seeing cigarettes as cool, think about having black lungs and wrinkly skin. Instead of blowing up at your little brother, think about how you will be the one who gets in trouble for losing your temper. (This is what the preschoolers did when they turned the marshmallow into something undesirable.)

5. *Response Modulation*: Resisting temptation by using willpower. This is the least effective strategy, because at the moment of temptation it takes a lot of effort to resist. But it's one you can train yourself to succeed in when all else fails, if you keep your grit goal in mind. (This is what the preschoolers did when they stared at the marshmallow and said to themselves, *Don't eat it.*)

Let's see how Rachel, a college sophmore, uses self-control strategies to grow her academic grit.

Rachel wishes she got better grades, but she finds it hard to stay focused on her schoolwork and is easily distracted by text messages or updates on social media. The good news is that Rachel is motivated to change: she is eager to join her friends on the school's study-abroad program, for which she needs at least a B+ average.

Process Model of Self-Control Strategies

Strategy	Example
Choose to be in a situation that ignores impulses and promotes desires. (Situation Selection)	Rachel can go to the library to do her homework, where she will be less tempted to use or talk on her phone.
Change the circumstances of the situation to ignore impulses and promote desires. (Situation Modification)	If she needs to work in her room, Rachel can turn off websites that might distract her, or turn off her Wi-Fi altogether.
Focus your attention in ways that avoid temptation or make you more mindful of your choices. (Attention Deployment)	Rachel can shut off her phone or put it someplace—like the closet—where she can't see it while she's working.
Change thinking about the choice to recognize the negatives of impulses and the benefits of long-term goals. (Cognitive Change)	Rachel can remind herself how insignificant Snapchatting is compared to how good it will feel to raise her GPA and join her friends on the study-abroad program.
In the moment, just resist temptation by using willpower and suppressing impulses. (Response Modulation)	The next time Rachel finds herself wanting to take a break while working, she can double down on her work and get busy instead of checking her phone. (This is probably the least effective strategy.)

for you to do

1. Think about the grit domain where you are already gritty (your grit strength). Do you rely on willpower or do you use some of the strategies listed early on in the chart?

_____

2. What self-control strategies, either ones from the chart or ones you have discovered yourself, are you using to be successful in this area?

_____

3. Now, thinking about your grit goal, answer the following questions.

   How much do you rely on willpower?

   _____

   What strategies might you use that would be more effective?

   _____

let's dig deeper

Over the next week, commit to using effective self-control strategies to address your grit goal. See if you can avoid using the last one—response modulation or willpower. List the self-control strategies you will use here.

_____

_____

_____

We are what we repeatedly do. Excellence, then, is not an act, but a habit.

—Aristotle

for you to know

When we look closely at the behavior of gritty people, we can see that they are not exerting self-control or using willpower all day long—that would be exhausting! Rather, they are engaging in *habits* that promote grit.

As we discussed in the previous activity, we all do better when we set ourselves up for success as opposed to trying to use willpower in the face of temptation. Willpower is a limited resource;[40] you can get only so far by muscling your way through temptation (for example, *I won't eat the marshmallow… I won't eat the marshmallow…*). However, when an activity becomes a habit, it is automatic and no longer needs to draw upon your limited resource of willpower.

For example, I have gotten into the habit of getting up early to write this workbook. Although it was hard at first, once it became a habit it was easier to do because it became *automatic*. To make your gritty behavior really stick, you need to make it a habit.

All habits exist because there is a cue, a routine, and a reward.[41]

For example, when you procrastinate, it starts with a *cue*—the feeling of *I have so much work to do!*

The *routine* is *you delay starting your work.*

The *reward* is *you feel better in the moment because you avoided something that made you feel uncomfortable.*

This cycle creates a *habit loop.* Unfortunately, though, the short-term reward of avoiding discomfort results in a long-term cost—your work's still not done.

When you change a habit, the cue stays the same (*I have so much work*) and the reward results naturally, so what you need to change is *the routine.* The cue helps you identify when you are about to fall into an old habit, but this time you create a *new habit or routine* instead.

Let's continue with this example.

The *cue* is still the *stressful feeling* of having a lot of work.

But you can establish a *new routine* by getting started right away.

And the *new reward* is that you will have your work done, have more free time later, and you won't feel so stressed by the undone work hanging over your head.

Changing habits is hard. Our brains are lazy, and unless we deliberately create a new routine, we will follow a bad habit automatically. The good news is, if you are diligent and consistent in creating new routines, these new routines will one day be as automatic as your old bad habits.

for you to do:

1. Write down one bad habit that is interfering with your grit goal (*grit goal: emotional grit; bad habit: losing my temper.*)

   _____

2. What is the *cue*? (*I lose my temper whenever my parents nag me about doing my homework.*)

   _____

3. What is the *routine*? (*I yell at my parents and avoid getting started on my homework.*)

   _____

4. What is the *reward* for this bad habit? (*I feel better because I have avoided starting my homework. Plus, yelling releases my anger and makes me feel good in the moment.*)

   _____

5. Write down one new good habit you would like to create that will support your gritty behavior. (*I will stay calm when my parents nag me about homework.*)

   _____

6. What is the *cue*? (Same as the bad habit cue—*My parents nag me about getting things done.*)

   _____

7. What is the *new routine*? (*I will remind myself that my parents and I are on the same team. Their nagging may be annoying, but they are trying to help. Plus, if I start my homework when they ask me to, I can avoid a fight and the crash that comes after I lose my temper.*)

   _____

8. What is the *new reward* of this good, new habit? (*I will feel proud that I had better self-control, my parents will get off my back, and the work will get done.*)

   _____

Here are some tips to keep this new habit of yours effective.

1. *Make it easy to engage in the new habit and hard to engage in the old habit.* In his book *Before Happiness: Five Actionable Strategies to Create a Positive Path to Success,* psychologist Shawn Achor writes about wanting to develop the habit of running more and watching less television. So what did he do? He took the batteries out of his remote control and slept in his running clothes.[42] Think about what you can do to make it easier to achieve the habit you want. For example, put your flute case on the floor next to your bed so you'll remember to practice first thing in the morning, and move your phone to a room far away from you so it won't distract you while you work.

2. *Be specific and don't take on too much.* It's tough enough to change one habit, so don't try to change more than one at a time. For example, don't take on exercising, being emotionally gritty, and procrastinating less all at the same time. When you have identified the behavior you want to change, break the change down into small, manageable steps so it doesn't seem overwhelming.[43] (This is why I asked you to start with SMART goals—goals that are small, manageable, and specific.)

3. *Write it down and monitor yourself.* Science has shown that writing down what we want to accomplish is more effective than just saying it.[44] Instead of thinking *I have to get my work done,* make a schedule and write it down: "Sunday 9 to 10: finish math homework; 11 to 12: physics; 12 to 1: lunch; 1 to 2: go to the gym." Remember the activity 13 tip to write down your goals? Same idea.

4. *Stand firm; no wavering.* One way you can be sure to stick with a habit is to tell yourself that there is no other choice.[45] Try to create rules for yourself, like *I will not go on Facebook until I have finished my homework.* Once you start having an internal dialogue, like *I'll just spend a few minutes checking my phone,* you have lost the battle! It's best to commit in advance and be like the Nike ad: "Just do it!"

5. *Don't overreact when you mess up.* Everyone messes up sometimes. But sometimes when people get off track they overreact and turn a small problem into a bigger one.[46] For example, if you watch a YouTube video when you're supposed to be studying, you might think, *I might as well blow off the whole night.* However, this

makes no sense. Psychologist Judith Beck provides a great analogy: "If you fell down one step, would you fall down all the rest?" Obviously not! So why would you act this way in terms of growing your grit? You can acknowledge the lapse, but give yourself *credit* for getting back on track.

6. *Anticipate challenges and plan for obstacles.* In her book, *Better than Before*, Gretchen Rubin discusses the importance of anticipating and planning for your triggers.[47] One way to do this is to use what Peter Gollowitzer calls an "if-then plan."[48] For example, if I get distracted by my phone, then I will go to the library without my phone. When you make an if-then plan, you are not making decisions in the moment, when you can be easily tempted. Instead, you are just following a plan that was previously committed to, using long-term thinking.

7. *Reward often.* Rewards are necessary to change and sustain habits. Especially when a habit is being formed (the hardest part), rewards can help. If you want your willpower to last, reward yourself often.

Let's hear Katie and Kira's (high school seniors) favorite habits that grow their grit.

- Stay in the front row in school or in an exercise class.

- Use a schedule for schoolwork (and if the schedule needs to change, get back on track rather than abandoning the schedule).

- Study somewhere other than your bedroom (your bedroom has too many distractions).

- Only check e-mail/social media at the beginning and end of the day (not all day long). When doing work, make the screen full size and turn off all other distractions (e-mail, Facebook, and so on). Set aside time every day for yourself (ideally before bed) without technology/distractions.

- When you're stressed, take a deep breath before you react to anything.

- Wait ten seconds before giving in to a temptation or making an emotional decision (for example, giving up at the gym or lashing out at a sibling).

---

let's dig deeper

What strategies will you use to support your new habit? Circle *three* on this list.

1. Make it easy to engage in the new habit and hard to engage in the old habit.

2. Be specific, and don't take on too much.

3. Write it down and monitor.

4. Stand firm: no wavering.

5. Don't overreact when problems arise.

6. Anticipate challenges and make an if-then plan for obstacles.

7. Reward often.

let's review our gritty behavior 18

Knowing is not enough; we must apply. Willing is not enough; we must do.

—Johann von Goethe

In this chapter, you have learned ways to develop gritty behavior—the next step in achieving your grit goal.

Let's see how well you have understood key gritty behavior concepts. Keeping your grit goal in mind:

1. Did you set five specific, measurable, and achievable *SMART goals?*

   Yes ☐   *Not yet* ☐

2. Did you apply *deliberate practice* to the SMART goal(s) that were giving you trouble or standing in your way?

   Yes ☐   *Not yet* ☐

3. Did you put your goals at the forefront of your mind by making *Advantage Cards* and reading them every day?

   Yes ☐   *Not yet* ☐

4. Were you able to assert more *self-control* by avoiding temptations and cognitively reframing temptation, rather than just using willpower?

   Yes ☐   *Not yet* ☐

5. Did you take steps to turn your gritty behavior into a *habit*?

   Yes ☐   *Not yet* ☐

Congratulations! You are doing great. Be sure to savor your success and give yourself credit for everything you have accomplished. The final chapter will help you deal with any obstacles you might still be facing so you can finish strong.

CHAPTER 4

Overcoming Barriers to Grit

Grit is living life like it's a marathon, not a sprint.

—Angela Duckworth

In this chapter, you will learn strategies to help you overcome *barriers to grit*—those moments when, despite the progress you've made, you may just feel like giving up. If the journey toward grit can be compared to a twenty-six-mile marathon, think of yourself as being at mile 20.

The strategies in this chapter will help you find the extra strength you need to get to the finish line; they combine thinking with doing (mind-set with behavior). Specifically, in this chapter I will show you how to:

1. Connect to your *values* and *find a higher purpose*. By doing so you will find the passion you need to fully develop your grit goal.

2. Focus on the present moment (*mindfulness*) and see the good (*gratitude*) in order to further strengthen your perseverance.

3. *Cope effectively with stress*, which can interfere with building grit.

4. Reach out to other people and *build a community of grit*, because becoming grittier is a team effort.

My goal in this chapter is to give you the tools you need to finish strong. In an exercise class I take, the instructor often likes to end with what he calls "finishers"—high-intensity exercises that push you just a smidge more, right at the point when you feel ready to give up. The point of finishers is to show you that your muscles can do even more than you thought they could so that you leave class feeling stronger, more confident, and energized. That's how I would like you to feel after *finishing* this chapter—stronger, more energized and confident so you can go from *good* to *great*.

connecting to your values and finding a sense of purpose

It's only when you hitch your wagon to something larger than yourself that you realize your true potential and discover the role that you'll play in writing the next great chapter in the American story.

—Barack Obama

for you to know

Imagine you are running that marathon and, after twenty miles, you hit the infamous "wall." (For all you nonrunners, the wall is a point at which many runners feel like they can't go on.) What can you do?

Maybe you can think about why running this race was *important to you* in the first place.

Or maybe, if you are running the race for a charity or cause, you can focus on how the race will *help others*.

To finish your grit goal strong—and push through any walls you might be facing—you will need to dig deep. One way to do that is by connecting to your values and passion (identifying your core values) or connecting your grit goal to something larger than yourself (a purpose). Research has shown that doing this increases persistence, resilience, and well-being—all factors that contribute to grit.[49]

Connecting to Your Core Values

Aligning your grit goal to a core value is one way to keep going when things get tough. A core value—a concept discussed in activity 5—is a principle or standard (such as courage or faith) that you can use to guide your actions because it is something you want to live up to.[50]

Let's see how Tom uses his core values of *caring* and *family* to fuel his academic grit.

Tom's parents want him to be the first person in their family to graduate from college. They work two jobs in order to provide him with the best education. Tom loves his parents and appreciates all that they have done for him; they have served as models of love and perseverance and, based on their actions, he too hopes to graduate from college. But like all teens, Tom sometimes would rather hang out with his friends than study. However, his core values of honoring his parents' sacrifices and fulfilling the goal they share redirect him when he is tempted to skip class or his schoolwork. At those times, Tom thinks about not only how his parents would feel if he cut class, but also how he would feel knowing he had let them down. In this way, Tom's core values of caring and love of family help him work toward his grit goal even in the face of temptation.

Finding a Higher Purpose

Often, people who are exemplars of grit don't act gritty just for themselves. Their behavior and effort serve a larger purpose.[51]

What do I mean by purpose? Having purpose is defined as "an intention to accomplish something that is at the same time *meaningful to the self* and consequential *for the world beyond the self*.[52] In other words, purpose is having a goal that you care deeply about and that benefits the world at large (like bringing joy to others, or caring for the environment). Having purpose allows you to be both *persistent* in your long-term goal and *resilient* when you have setbacks, because you feel inspired by that higher meaning.

At my son's high school graduation, one of the teachers, Yoram Roschwalb, offered this advice: "Rather than working to be the best in the world at something, aim to be the best for the world." In the same vein, when Simone Manuel became the first African-American woman to win an individual Olympic gold medal in swimming at the 2016 Olympics in Rio, she said, "The gold medal wasn't just for me. It was for people who came before me and inspired me to stay in this sport, and for people who believe that they can't do it."[53] It is clear from Simone's statement that she connected her swimming and training to a *higher purpose*. She worked hard and trained not only for herself but for other African-American girls both before and after her who might be motivated and inspired by her. This is what purpose is all about!

Let's see how Diego connects his love of music to a higher purpose:

Diego loves to play the piano, and he especially enjoys playing for the nursing home residents he visits once a month. Even though he loves playing, practicing can be draining, especially when he needs to go over one section of music again and again. When Diego needs to find the motivation to practice, he thinks about how much he loves music, and he thinks about how much joy his music brings to the people at the nursing home. In his way, connecting his music to a higher purpose helps Diego be gritty.

for you to do

Read the following core values. Which ones matter the most to you? Which ones guide your decisions? Which ones do you appreciate about yourself? If another value comes to mind that is not on the list, write it down.

Achievement	Faith	Independence
Adventure	Family	Leadership
Caring	Friendship	Learning
Community	Fun	Loyalty
Courage	Happiness	Peace
Creativity	Health	Responsibility
Curiosity	Honesty	Work
Fairness	Humor	Wisdom

Choose your top values and write about them. When writing about each value, try to answer the following questions:

What does this value mean to me? Why is this value important to me? How did I learn this value? How do I express this value in my life?

_____

_____

_____

_____

_____

_____

_____

_____

Now try using a core value to assist you in developing your grit goal. For example, say you are working on growing your emotional grit, and you have the core values of happiness and caring. How might these values inspire you to be more emotionally gritty?

_____

_____

_____

let's dig deeper

Answering these questions will help you discover the *higher purpose* for your grit goal.[54]

Ask yourself:

Why does my grit goal matter to me?

_____

What do I hope to accomplish *for myself and others* with my effort? Why is this important?

_____

How could my grit goal make a positive contribution to society or to something larger than myself?

_____

How would the world be a better place if I became grittier in this area?

_____

It may be hard to find a higher purpose for your grit goal. If you haven't found it, remember to keep a growth mind-set: you just haven't found it.

Remember, when you combine passion with *purpose* you can overcome obstacles and break through barriers!

encouraging mindfulness and gratitude 20

Between stimulus and response there is a space. In that space is our power to choose our response. In our response lies our growth and our freedom.

—Victor Frankl

You may be wondering, *How are mindfulness and gratitude related to grit, and how can they give me the extra push I need to finish strong?*

When you are mindful, you are able to focus on the present moment with kindness, compassion, and reflection—all necessary to creating a gritty mind-set. When you are mindful, you are able to be more thoughtful and deliberate—necessary steps to growing gritty behavior.

When you feel gratitude, you can reframe your thinking to see the good. And as you know from previous activities, being optimistic will help you persist and bounce back from challenges and setbacks.

Being mindful and grateful are worthwhile tools to grow your grit and finish strong.

being mindful

What is mindfulness?

Scientist Jon Kabat-Zinn, a leader in the field of mindfulness, says, "Mindfulness is paying attention in the present moment, with kindness, a lack of judgment, compassion, and curiosity, and responding rather than reacting to circumstance." In other words, being mindful is being aware of the present moment without judgment and without trying to change it. Mindfulness is staying focused on one thing at a time and not letting future events or past failures overwhelm you. When you are mindful, you are able to create a space between what you are feeling and how you react. In that space, you are able to make good decisions.

How is mindfulness connected to grit? Practicing mindfulness:

1. Puts you in charge of your mind instead of letting your mind be in charge of you.

2. Lets you act more thoughtfully and less impulsively.

3. Helps you see reality more accurately so you can avoid thinking traps.

4. Reduces stress and increases well-being and positive emotions.

5. Helps you pause before you react to a situation or emotion, which is essential when you need to persist and rebound from setbacks.

6. Teaches you to approach a challenge from a curious place as opposed to a judgmental one.

for you to do

Here are two ways to increase your mindfulness.

- *The chocolate kiss exercise* (modified from the raisin exercise because I like chocolate much more than raisins, but you can pick any small treat). Hold the chocolate kiss in your hand. Use all five senses (seeing, hearing, smelling, touching, tasting) to experience the chocolate kiss as you slowly bring it to your mouth. (Leave tasting it to the end.) If thoughts come into your head, simply acknowledge them and let them float away as you return your attention to the chocolate kiss and the present moment.

- *Mindfulness during everyday activities.* Practice mindfulness while engaging in everyday activities such as walking your dog, brushing your teeth, or taking a shower. During these activities, bring your full attention to the present moment. Notice the physical sensations and try to activate all your senses (touch, taste, sight, sound, and smell). If thoughts arise, try to see these thoughts as clouds going by or leaves floating down a river and return to the task at hand.

Both of these activities train your brain to be more thoughtful, present-oriented, and reflective, all of which are essential for grit.

cultivating gratitude

What is gratitude?

We often spend too much time thinking about what is going wrong in our lives and not enough thinking about everything that is going right. Although we can learn and grow by reflecting on bad events, we often dwell on them rather than learning from them. One way to combat this natural tendency is to think about what we are grateful for.

With gratitude, we acknowledge the goodness in our lives and the contribution of others to our happiness.[55] Gratitude is important for building grit because it helps you persist and be more resilient; if you focus on what is working, you are more likely to stick with it. Being grateful allows you to find the silver lining in a challenge, which makes it easier to get back on track. For example, if you are working on being socially grittier, being grateful for the person who smiled at you will help you keep going more than focusing on the person who did not notice you. No matter what area you are working on, being grateful for the progress you've made will help you more than focusing on what you have not accomplished *yet*.

Being grateful also allows you to cope more effectively with stress and increase your resilience. When we are grateful, we are able to find more *meaning and purpose* in our lives—all of which helps increase our grit!

for you to do

Here are two ways to increase your gratitude:

- Write a letter to someone you have never properly thanked for their positive influence in your life—a parent, a teacher, a friend.[56] Let the person know the specific things you are grateful for. You can send an e-mail or text, but it is most *powerful* if you read your letter of gratitude in person. You will be surprised how much the other person—and *you*—will get out of this activity.

- Keep a gratitude journal, in which you write down the things you are grateful for each day—a beautiful sunrise, a good night's sleep, hearing your favorite song on the radio. Gratitude journaling slowly changes the way we perceive situations by adjusting what we focus on. When we focus on what is good and special in our lives, those things rise to the top (remember the red experiment from activity 15?).

When completing these activities, try to savor the feelings of gratitude that you have for all the goodness in your life. Let the good feelings sink in "like the sun's warmth into a T-shirt, water into a sponge, or a jewel placed in a treasure chest in your heart."[57] Take a mental picture of these grateful moments so that you can access them during times of challenge.

let's dig deeper

Combining Mindfulness with Gratitude: Breath of Thanks[58]

1. Notice how your breath flows in and out without your having to do anything. Continue breathing this way. Try to slow your breathing down.

2. With each of the next five to eight exhalations, silently say the words *thank you* to remind yourself of the gift of breath and how lucky you are to be alive. Practice this activity two or three times a day and at least three times per week.

When engaging in these activities, did you notice an uptick in positive feelings? Were you able to be more reflective and thoughtful? Do you think these strategies will help grow your grit?

Cultivating positive emotions by engaging in mindfulness and gratitude is important, but thinking about the flip side—coping with negative feelings—is also essential. The next activity will help you cope with stress.

coping with stress 21

Stress is like spice—in the right proportion it enhances the flavor of a dish.
Too little produces a bland, dull meal; too much may choke you.

—Donald Tubesing

for you to know

When we are stressed, we are more reactive, less thoughtful, and more likely to choose what feels good in the moment. As you have learned, to be gritty we need to do the exact opposite! That's why I say stress is kryptonite to grit.

Stress at any age can interfere with the brain's ability to exhibit grit, but it has a particularly powerful impact on teenagers. That's because of how the teenage brain develops. Our emotions are controlled by two parts of the brain: the amygdala (the fight-or-flight part that reacts quickly to perceived threats) and the frontal lobe (the part that controls and regulates emotions). When you were younger, these two parts developed evenly. However, with the onset of puberty, your amygdala starts to grow exponentially, while the frontal lobe does not. In fact, the frontal lobe does not catch up to the amygdala until you are in your mid-twenties![59] This lopsided development makes it particularly difficult for teenagers to manage and control stress.

Sometimes a degree of stress actually "enhances the flavor of a dish." And sometimes you just can't avoid stress. Your best option is to reframe the cause of your stress. (Remember, how we think about an event affects how we feel about it.) Try thinking of stress as a way to boost performance (*my heart's racing can energize me*) or as a way to grow (*stress is a sign that my brain is growing*) and succeed (*no one succeeds without some stress along the way*).[60] By facing challenging or stressful situations, you will become stronger and more adept at handling similar situations in the future.

So in order to be gritty, especially at your age, you need to learn how to reframe and cope with stress. Here are my top ten ways to cope effectively with stress:

1. *Be a detective.* Learn to recognize, as a detective would, when stress is creeping up on you. For example, where do you feel stress in your body? What thinking traps are you falling into? Recognizing that stress is interfering with your functioning, and your grittiness, is the first step to getting it under control.

2. *Get your brain back.* When we are stressed, we go into fight-or-flight mode. In this state, adrenaline courses through our veins and makes it hard for us to think clearly. Before you can change your relationships with stress, you need to reduce stress hormones. Exercising, such as doing jumping jacks or shooting baskets, can use up some of those stress hormones. Some people even find that splashing their face with cold water helps them disengage from stress. Although it sounds simple, breathing slowly can also be an effective stress reducer by allowing you to be more reflective. Lastly, having good eating and sleeping habits, long-term fixes, are also essential to reducing stress and getting your brain back.

3. *Assess the situation accurately.* Make sure you are seeing the problem for what it is and not blowing it up into something it's not. Ask yourself: *Is this an ant problem or a dinosaur problem?* Or: *Is this a real tiger or a paper (imaginary) tiger?*

4. *Notice and challenge those thinking traps.* See if you have fallen into any thinking traps, such as awfulizing (activity 7) or are engaging in the Problematic P's— making it personal, pervasive, and permanent (activity 8). If so, take note of your thinking, challenge it, and come up with ways of thinking that both are true and support your new gritty behavior.

5. *Reappraise and reframe the situation.* Can you reframe the stressful experience and use it as a way to energize and invigorate you, to "enhance the flavor of your dish"?

6. *Develop a growth mind-set.* Ask yourself, *What can I learn from this stressful event? How can I grow?* In the words of Martin Luther King, Jr., "Only when it is dark enough can you see the stars."

7. *Break the situation down into manageable steps.* You learned this approach when you made SMART goals. To use the marathon metaphor, don't think about the twenty-six miles to go; instead, just focus on putting one foot in front of the other.

8. *Watch out for suppression.* Telling yourself *Don't be stressed!* actually makes you feel more stressed. It's like telling yourself, *Don't think about pink elephants.* What happens? All you can think about are pink elephants! Instead, acknowledge the worry thoughts and picture them as clouds going by or leaves floating down a river.

9. *Be kind to others and to yourself.* When we are kind to others and show compassion (not judgment), we experience greater happiness and well-being (antidotes to stress). Being kind to yourself and others helps you reduce fear, feel safe, and pursue your long-term dreams.[61] (More about this in activity 22.)

10. *Get support.* We all do best when we have people we can count on to help us manage stressful events. Having at least one person who stands by you and believes in you is a key factor in coping with stress and building resilience.[62] (More about this in activity 22.)

Let's see how Jayden uses these ten methods to fight stress and improve his academic grit.

When my teachers correct my school work, and my first response is to feel overwhelmed and shut down. However, whenever I get that feeling, I remind myself that it's the stress talking. I take a deep breath and remind myself that their feedback is an "ant problem," not a "dinosaur problem." I try to take a walk around the room or roll my neck in circles while breathing slowly to help me think more clearly. I remember that my teachers are giving me this feedback so that I can grow and because they have high expectations for me. Also, instead of focusing on all of the red marks on the page, I look at each comment one at a time. I remind myself that the teachers aren't judging me, but are there to help me grow. By thinking this way, I am able to better manage my stress and be academically grittier.

for you to do

One technique to reduce stress is *self-distancing*.[63] When we create space between ourselves and what is stressing us, we can think more thoughtfully and reflectively and be grittier. In self-distancing, we make a separation in time (not now), in space (not here), hypothetically (not real), and from ourselves, seeing the stress affecting someone else (not me).

1. Think about a stressful event. It could be an important exam, or going to a meeting or event where you don't know a lot of people.

2. Write it down.

   _____

3. Try to visualize the stressful experience as though you are going through it (*you* are taking the exam or *you* are at the meeting). Let the feelings of stress come through you.

4. Now, let's try some self-distancing. Take a step back and watch the scene play out as if you were watching a movie. Or try to visualize the experience as if you were watching from the balcony or as a "fly on the wall." See if you can use your name instead of "I" when thinking about the stressful event.[64] For example, "Why did Caren feel this way?" Instead of, "Why did I feel this way?"

Does taking a step back help you view the situation differently?

Another way to distance yourself from a stressful situation is to ask yourself what you would say to a friend who was going through the same thing. Can you give the advice you might give a friend to yourself instead?

let's dig deeper

The previous activities were mind-set strategies to address stress. The following are behavioral strategies to address stress. Remember, combining mind-set with behavior is the key to change.

Breath Counting: 3:5 Ratio

Try this breathing technique for at least a minute, or as long as you like. Count to three as you inhale through your nose, then count to five as you exhale through your mouth.

Finger Breathing (a version of Breath Counting)

Hold up one hand in front of you, palm facing toward you. With the index finger of your other hand, trace up the outside of your thumb while you inhale (counting to three), pausing at the top of your thumb. Then trace down the other side while you exhale (counting to five). Then, trace up the side of the next finger while you inhale, pause at the top, and trace down the other side while you exhale. Keep going, tracing along each finger as you count through each breath. When you get to the outer base of your pinky, come back up that finger and retrace your steps.

This practice gives you something to do with your hands as you breathe and count. It can be useful when it is hard to close your eyes and when you need something to ground you.

Did you know that when we are stressed, we have a desire to reach out to others?[65] In the next activity, I will show you how reaching out to others can help you manage stress and grow your grit!

22 finding your cheerleader and building a community of grit

To the world you may be one person, but to one person you may be the world.

—Unknown

for you to know

Up until now, you have grown your grit mostly by focusing on changing *yourself—your* mind-set and behavior. However, this is not the whole picture. As important as your internal work has been, it is equally important that you reach out to other people and build a community of grit.

Teens often tell me that their connections to other people are what help them stay gritty and persevere in the face of obstacles. Here are some of their answers to the question, "How do you stay gritty?"

I talk to a friend or teacher.

I ask someone for a hug.

I surround myself with positive energy.

I reach out to my people.

This isn't only true for humans. Did you know that mother rats that lick their pups (a form of bonding for rats) raise braver, more curious, and more resilient rats?[66] Although I am not suggesting you get licked, I *am* suggesting that you build connections with others so you have someone in your corner when the going gets tough.

Find Your Cheerleader

Human beings thrive when they know they're in a
secure place where other people truly respect them.

—Angela Duckworth

Research shows that having a charismatic adult—someone from whom you gather strength—can be the key to coping with stress[67] and building perseverance, because when we connect with others we have better attention, better emotional regulation, and better immune functioning. This social connection can be a parent, a teacher, a big brother or sister, or a special uncle or aunt. Having individuals who are supportive and an environment that you can trust will both allow you to ignore the siren of instant gratification and give you the inner strength to move successfully through obstacles toward a better and more fulfilling future.

Connecting with others and building strong relationships will also help you forge a sense of belonging.[68] When we feel we belong, we are more likely to be invested and persevere and less likely to withdraw and become pessimistic.

Having an accountability partner can also be helpful. Your accountability partner assists you not only by giving you support but also by not allowing you to stray from your grit goal. This person could be a teenage friend or an adult, but should be someone who can *keep you on your toes*. Your partner will be available to swap ideas with you and help you overcome your obstacles and stick to your inner values and higher purpose.

Be a Cheerleader for Others

Did you know that *giving help* can grow your perseverance? We all possess an inborn desire to help. In my school, for example, one of the most coveted classroom

117

jobs a kindergartener can get is to be teacher's helper for the day. And that passion for helping does not go away when you're a teen. Think about a time you helped someone else. How did it make you feel? If you are like most people, helping other people enhances feelings of positivity, which makes it easier to be more persistent and resilient—in a word, gritty.

Also, helping others can get your mind off of your own struggles. By noticing that other people need help, their needs become more important than your own. When your awareness moves to another person, your perspective expands, and your own problems seem smaller.

Develop a Community of Grit

Gritty people don't have just *one* person they can count on. They are surrounded by a community of grit, a place where individuals come together to motivate and ignite each other's passions and purpose. For both good and bad, we have a strong drive to conform to and imitate the behavior of others. So when you surround yourself with gritty people, you are more likely to be gritty yourself. Conversely, you probably already know there are some people you'd best avoid, because they distract you from growing your grit.

I see this when I'm at the gym, working to stay gritty with my wellness. When I see people around me taking shortcuts (modifying their pushups or slowing their pace), it becomes easier for me to do the same in my own routines. But when they're working hard, I get inspired to stay on task and finish strong.

Why is this? You may know that you have neurons in your brain that inform you about emotions. But did you know that you also have *mirror neurons*,[69] which reflect— or "mirror back"—the emotions of the people around you? So if you are around people who are stressed, you are more likely to feel stressed; if you are around people who are smiling, you are more likely to feel happy yourself; and when you spend time with gritty people, their passion and perseverance rub off on you. Emotions are contagious!

for you to do

Who can you enlist to be your cheerleaders—people who can help you when you are struggling with your grit goal?

_____

_____

_____

Who can be your grit accountability partner—someone who can keep you on your toes when you feel like giving up?

_____

How can you be a cheerleader to others? Can you provide support to someone else?

_____

_____

_____

Can you volunteer (help others) for a cause that is important to you?

_____

let's dig deeper

How can you cultivate a community of grit?

_____

_____

Whose actions will positively affect you?

_____

_____

Are there people who need to be avoided?

_____

_____

How can you get involved with people who share your passion and display a high degree of grit? (For example, join your school's baseball team, or hang out with people who are outgoing or academically invested.)

_____

_____

Grit is not just a simple elbow-grease term for rugged persistence. It is an often invisible display of endurance that lets you stay in an uncomfortable place, work hard to improve upon a given interest, and do it again and again.

—Sarah Lewis

for you to know

One of the grittiest people I can think of is Dorothy from *The Wizard of Oz*. She had a long-term goal (getting back to Kansas) that she was passionate about. She kept her goal front and center despite many obstacles (a poisonous poppy field, a wicked witch, flying monkeys). Throughout her journey, she maintained a positive outlook, and when she got stuck, she asked for help from her network of friends who encouraged her to be thoughtful (the Scarecrow), courageous (the Lion), and to always have heart (the Tin Man). With their support and her own grit, Dorothy created a gritty community, one that ultimately helped her accomplish her goal: to return home.

Just like Dorothy, you are almost home! At this point, you have accomplished a lot in terms of growing your grit. Although you weren't dodging witches and flying monkeys, you have learned how to dig deep to unlock your inner strength by tapping into mind-set and behavioral strategies. When that was not enough, you reached out to people who helped you find the tools to make your dreams come true. And, lastly, by strengthening an area that you cared about improving—your grit goal—you have developed skills that will last a lifetime.

I hope that you can *now* answer with confidence the following "P" questions:

What is my *passion*?

How can I *persist* with my grit goal?

How can I *persevere* in the face of setbacks?

Can I tie my grit goal to a larger *purpose*?

And ultimately—can I answer in the affirmative that *grit pays off*?

for you to do

The Grit Survey Revisited

Look back at the survey you took in activity 2, and see how much your grit has grown.

What was your grit score originally? (Refer to question 1 from the survey.) _____

What is your grit score now? _____

What was your original grit score in the domain you have been working on? (Refer to your answers to questions 5 through 9, depending on the domain you selected.) _____

What is your grit score in that domain now? (Refer to your answers to questions 5 through 9, depending on the domain you selected.) _____

Has your overall grit score gone up? Has the domain you identified as your grit goal gotten stronger?

> *Yes* ☐   *Not yet* ☐

Looking at questions 2, 3, and 4 in the grit survey, have you gained a *gritty mind-set*, started practicing *gritty behavior*, and learned how to *break through barriers* and *overcome obstacles* to grit?

> *Yes* ☐   *Not yet* ☐

Don't worry if your scores haven't gone up. Research shows that when you are actively growing your grit (as you have been doing in this workbook), your own assessment of your grit can go down as you become more aware of the process and hold yourself to higher standards.[70] In other words, you become grittier with yourself and rate yourself lower! So don't focus too much on the numbers, but know that you have taken steps to become grittier.

Now, look back at activity 3, where you identified your grit strengths and weaknesses. Do you notice that you are now applying the strategies you were naturally using in your grit strength to your grit goal?

List one strategy from your grit strength that you are using with your grit goal.

_____

Learning from your strengths and being open to new and effective strategies are keys to building success.

let's dig deeper

One of the themes of this chapter is that helping others helps you. With this in mind, imagine that a family member or friend is struggling with grit. Take a few minutes to reflect on your process; then write a letter to this person, sharing your growth in both your mind-set and your behavior.

For example:

Dear Aunt Julianna,

I wanted to write and let you know how I overcame my struggles with being emotionally gritty. I hope it will help you with your desire to be grittier in terms of your health.

I started by understanding why it was important for me to be stronger in this area. I made specific goals and kept practicing until I got better. I still fall into thinking traps sometimes, but when I do, I challenge them. Getting help from my older sister and telling my friends about my goal has made a lot of difference. I also practice meditation and keep a gratitude journal. I know you too can be grittier with your goal of grit health. Maybe you could find a walking buddy or join a gym. I would love to help you.

Love always,

Your niece

Now you try.

_____

_____

_____

_____

_____

_____

_____

You can do incredible things when you have grit. By combining passion with perseverance and having people who support you, you can achieve more than you ever imagined!

Thank you for taking this journey with me. And, remember—if your grit isn't where you want it to be, it is just not there *yet!*

Acknowledgments

If I have seen further than others, it is by standing upon the shoulders of giants.

—Sir Isaac Newton

This workbook would not be possible without the strong shoulders of many "giants" who have influenced my thinking. The enormous contributions of Angela Duckworth and her lab to the field of grit have served as the backdrop to this workbook. A special thank-you to my liaison from the Duckworth lab, David Meketon, who provided me with guidance and support. I had the privilege of studying with Walter Mischel at Barnard College, Columbia University, where he taught me to take laboratory discoveries and apply them to real life. I feel honored to be doing exactly that, both in my work as a psychologist and in the pages of this workbook. Thank you also to Robert Brooks, a staunch believer in the power of positive relationships to overcome obstacles and build resilience. Whenever I have felt stuck and in need of a charismatic adult, I could always count on him. Lastly, I feel privileged to have studied at the Albert Ellis Institute with Albert Ellis and Raymond DiGiuseppe, whose cognitive-behavioral principles have been critical to my thinking. The research of Carol Dweck and Martin Seligman has also greatly influenced this material. A special shout-out to the International Positive Education Network (IPEN). I am proud to be part of a movement dedicated to applying the science of well-being to all aspects of our lives. Thank you, Sir Anthony Seldon, for personally helping me to be grittier about eating fewer cookies after 9 p.m.

acknowledgments

Thank you to the many friends and colleagues who listened, read, provided feedback, and then reread what I wrote. Special thanks to Gil Noam, Toni Noble, K. Anders Ericsson, Arthur Schwartz, Gloria Schneider, Felisa Hochheiser, Marcia Mintz, Tobi Haims, Helene Walisever, Lauren Fahey, Mark Shinar, and Jennifer Horowitz for going beyond the call of duty.

One of the highlights of writing this workbook was working and speaking with teenagers who made sure that what I wrote would resonate with people their age. Thank you to Emily Weisbrot, Rachel Aboodi, Katie Parker, and Kira Cohen for your insight and expertise, and to everyone who shared their stories.

Thank you to the staff at New Harbinger and Kristi Hein for the edits, feedback, and more edits. I think we made a workbook that was better because of it. A special thank-you to Daisy Florin. I could not have done this project without you. Your ability to edit, prod, question, and push me is reflected in the workbook.

This workbook could not have been completed without the support of my teenage children, Corey and Emily. Thank you for letting me benignly neglect you while at the same time harassing you and your friends for input. Thank you Steve, my husband, for picking up the slack and providing insights and thoughtful edits along the way.

I feel blessed to have Elizabeth Brondolo as a mentor. You have significantly shaped both my thinking as a psychologist and the content of this workbook.

This workbook is dedicated to my father, Marcel Baruch, who was a paragon of grit. After spending much of World War II in a labor camp, he fulfilled his long-term goal of making a life for himself and his family first in Israel and then in America. No matter what obstacle he faced, he grew from it. Together with my mother, who is a shining light of optimism, passion, and positivity, he taught me to be gritty. Thank you, Mom and Dad, for always believing in me and raising me in an environment that supported passion, perseverance, and purpose.

Finally, I am grateful to you, the reader, for taking this journey with me. By giving to you, I gave to myself. The process has made me more optimistic, tenacious, and purposeful—in a word, grittier.

Notes

Introduction

1   A. Duckworth, *Grit: The Power of Passion and Perseverance* (New York: Scribner, 2016).

Activity 1

2   A. L. Duckworth, T. A. Kirby, Eli Tsukayama, H. Berstein, and K. A. Ericsson, "Deliberate Practice Spells Success: Why Grittier Competitors Triumph at the National Spelling Bee," *Social Psychological and Personality Science* 2 (2010): 174–181.

3   A. L. Duckworth, C. Peterson, M. D. Matthews, and D. R. Kelly, "Grit: Perseverance and Passion for Long-Term Goals," *Journal of Personality and Social Psychology* 92 (2007): 1087–1101.

4   Duckworth et al., "Grit: Perseverance and Passion," 1087. (Although "meaningful" is not part of Duckworth's original definition of *grit*, she has added it in recent discussions. This expanded definition is used throughout.)

5   Duckworth, *Grit*, The equations that follow also come from *Grit*, p. 42.

6   C. S. Dweck, "The Power of Believing That You Can Improve," November 2014, https://www.ted.com/talks/carol_dweck_the_power_.

Activity 2

7   V. J. Felitti and R. F. Anda, *The Adverse Childhood Experiences (ACE) Study*, Centers for Disease Control and Prevention, 1997, http://www.cdc.gov/ace/index.htm; W. Mischel, "Preference for Delayed Reinforcement: An Experimental Study of a Cultural Observation," *Journal of Abnormal and Social Psychology* 56 (1958): 57–61; N. Shechtman, A. H. DeBarger, C. Dornsife, S. Rosier, and L. Yarnall, *Promoting Grit, Tenacity, and Perseverance: Critical Factors for Success in the 21st Century* (Washington, DC: U.S. Department of Education Office of Educational Technology, 2013).

Activity 3

8 W. Mischel, Y. Shoda, and R. Mendoza-Denton, "Situation-Behavior Profiles as a Locus of Consistency in Personality," *Current Directions in Psychological Science* 11 (2002): 50–54; E. Tsukayama, A. L. Duckworth, and B. Kim, "Domain-Specific Impulsivity in School-age Children," *Developmental Science* 16 (2013): 879–893.

Activity 4

9 L. Winerman, *APA Monitor* 44, no. 11 (2015), http://www.apa.org/monitor/2013/12/high-achievers.aspx.

10 A. L. Duckworth and J. J. Gross, "Self-Control and Grit: Related but Separable Determinants of Success," *Current Directions in Psychological Science* 23 (2014): 319–325.

11 A. Tversky and D. Kahneman, "Loss Aversion in Riskless Choice: A Reference-Dependent Model," *Quarterly Journal of Economics* 106, no. 4 (1991): 1039–1061.

Activity 5

12 P. Brinol and R. Petty, "Overt Head Movements and Persuasion: A Self-Validation Analysis," *Journal of Personality and Social Psychology* 84 (2003): 1123–1139.

13 E. L. Deci and R. M. Ryan, *Intrinsic Motivation and Self-Determination in Human Behavior* (New York: Plenum, 1985).

14 Deci and Ryan, *Intrinsic Motivation*; D. S. Yeager, M. D. Henderson, D. Paunesku, G. M. Walton, S. D'Mello, B. J. Spitzer, and A. L. Duckworth, "Boring But Important: A Self-Transcendent Purpose for Learning Fosters Academic Self-Regulation," *Journal of Personality and Social Psychology* 107 (2014): 559–580.

15 D. K. Sherman and G. L. Cohen, *The Psychology of Self-Defense: Self-Affirmation Theory, Advances in Experimental Social Psychology*, ed. M. P. Zanna, vol. 38, pp. 183–242 (New York: Guildford Press, 2006); G. L. Cohen and D. K. Sherman, "The Psychology of Change: Self-Affirmation and Social Psychological Intervention," *Annual Review of Psychology* 65 (2014): 333–71.

16 W. Damon, *The Path to Purpose* (New York: Simon & Schuster, 2008); M. J. Poulin, E. A. Holman, and A. Buffone, "The Neurogenetics of Nice: Receptor Genes for Oxytocin and Vasopressin Interact with Threat to Predict Prosocial Behavior," *Psychological Science* 23 (2012): 446–52; Yeager et al., "Boring But Important."

Activity 6

17 R. Thaler, "Some Empirical Evidence on Dynamic Inconsistency," *Economics Letters* 8 (1981): 201–207.

18 D. Parfit, *Reasons and Persons* (New York: Oxford Press, 1986); D. M. Bartels and O. Urminsky, "On Intertemporal Selfishness: How the Perceived Instability of Identity Underlies Impatient Consumption," *Journal of Consumer Research* 38 (2011): 182–198.

19 D. Gilbert, *Stumbling on Happiness* (New York: Knopf, 2006).

20 Thaler (1981); H. E. Hershfield, D. G. Goldstein, W. F. Sharpe, J. Fox, J. L. Yeykelis, L. L. Carstensen, and J. N. Bailenson, "Increasing Saving Behavior Through Age-Progressed Renderings of the Future Self," *Journal of Marketing Research* 48 (2011): 23–37.

Activity 7

21 A. Ellis, *Overcoming Destructive Beliefs, Feelings, and Behaviors: New Directions for Rational Emotive Behavior Therapy* (New York: Prometheus Books, 2001).

Activity 8

22 A. L. Duckworth and L. Eskreis-Winkler, "True Grit," *Observer* 26 (2013): 1–3.

23 M. E. Seligman, K. Reivich, L. Jaycox, and J. Gillham, *The Optimistic Child* (Boston, MA: Houghton Mifflin, 1995).

24 M. E. Seligman, *Learned Optimism: How to Change Your Mind and Your Life* (New York: Knopf, 1991).

Activity 9

25 C. S. Dweck, *Mindset: How You Can Fulfill Your Potential* (New York: Random House, 2012).

26 Duckworth and Eskreis-Winkler, "True Grit."

27 Dweck, *Mindset*.

28 C. S. Dweck, "Recognizing and Overcoming False Growth Mindset," 2016, http://www.edutopia.org/blog/recognizing-overcoming-false-growth-mindset -carol-dweck.

Activity 10

29 C. S. Dweck, "The Power of Believing That You Can Improve," November 2014, https://www.ted.com/talks/carol_dweck_the_power_of_believing_that_you_can _improve.

Activity 11

30 J. C. Maxwell, *Failing Forward: Turning Mistakes into Stepping-Stones for Success* (Nashville, TN: Thomas Nelson, 2000).

Activity 13

31 G. T. Doran, "There's a S.M.A.R.T. Way to Write Management's Goals and Objectives," *Management Review* (AMA FORUM) 70 (1981): 35–36.

32 R. Hanson, *Hardwiring Happiness: The New Brain Science of Contentment, Calm, and Confidence* (New York: Harmony, 2013).

Activity 14

33. K. A. Ericsson, R. T. Krampe, and C. Tesch-Römer, "The Role of Deliberate Practice in the Acquisition of Expert Performance," *Psychological Review* 100 (1993): 363–406; K. A. Ericsson, *Peak: Secrets from the New Science of Expertise* (Boston: Houghton Mifflin Harcourt, 2016).

34 A. L. Duckworth, T. A. Kirby, E. Tsukayama, H. Berstein, and K. A. Ericsson, "Deliberate Practice Spells Success: Why Grittier Competitors Triumph at the National Spelling Bee," *Social Psychological and Personality Science*, 2 (2010): 174–181.

Activity 15

35 S. Fee, *Circle of F.R.I.E.N.D.S.* (Bothell, WA: Book Publishers Network, 2008).

36 J. Beck, *The Beck Diet Solution: Weight Loss Workbook* (Birmingham, AL: Oxmoor House, 2007).

Activity 16

37 W. Mischel, *The Marshmallow Test* (New York: Little, Brown, 2014).

38 A. L. Duckworth and J.J. Gross, "Self-Control and Grit: Related but Separable Determinants of Success," *Current Directions in Psychological Science* 23 (5) (2014): 1–7.

39 A. L. Duckworth, T. S. Gendler, and J. J Gross, "Self-Control in School-Age Children," *Educational Psychologist*, 49 (2014): 199–217.

Activity 17

40 R. F. Baumeister and J. Tierney, *Willpower: Rediscovering the Greatest Human Strength* (New York: Penguin Press, 2011).

41 C. Duhigg, *The Power of Habit: Why We Do What We Do in Life and Business* (New York: Random House, 2012).

42 S. Achor, *Before Happiness: Five Actionable Strategies to Create a Positive Path to Success* (New York: Crown Publishing Group, 2013).

43 S. Achor, *The Happiness Advantage: The Seven Principles of Positive Psychology That Fuel Success and Performance at Work* (New York: Broadway Books, 2010).

44 C. Heath and D. Heath, *Switch: How to Change Things When Change Is Hard* (New York: Broadway Books, 2010).

45 Beck, *The Beck Diet Solution*.

46 Beck, *The Beck Diet Solution*.

47 G. Rubin, *Better than Before* (New York: Broadway Books, 2015).

48 P. Gollowitzer, "Implementation Interventions: Strong Effects of Simple Plans," *American Psychologist* 54 (1999): 493–503.

Activity 19

49 Duckworth, *Grit*.

50 Cohen and Sherman, "The Psychology of Change" (2014); Sherman and Cohen, *The Psychology of Self-Defense* (2006); C. M. Steele, "The Psychology of Self-Affirmation: Sustaining the Integrity of the Self," *Advances in Experimental Social Psychology* 21 (1988): 261–302.

51 Duckworth, *Grit*; D. S. Yeager, M. J. Bundick, and R. Johnson, "The Role of Future Work Goal Motives in Adolescent Identity Development: A Longitudinal Mixed-Methods Investigation," *Contemporary Educational Psychology* 37 (2012): 206–17.

52 Damon, *The Path to Purpose*.

53 B. Svrluga, "Simone Manuel on making history: 'The gold medal wasn't just for me,'" *Washington Post* (August 11, 2016).

54 Damon, *The Path to Purpose*.

Activity 20

55 R. A. Emmons, *Thanks! How the New Science of Gratitude Can Make You Happier* (Boston: Houghton Mifflin, 2007).

56 M. E. Seligman, *Flourish: A Visionary New Understanding of Happiness and Well-Being* (New York: Free Press, 2012).

57 R. Hanson and R. Mendius, *Buddha's Brain: The Practical Neuroscience of Happiness, Love and Wisdom* (Oakland, CA: New Harbinger, 2009), 70.

58 F. Luskin, *Forgive for Good: A Proven Prescription for Health and Happiness* (San Francisco: Harper, 2002).

Activity 21

59 L. Steinberg, *Age of Opportunity: Lessons from the New Science of Adolescence* (Boston, MA: Eamon Dolan/Houghton Mifflin Harcourt, 2015).

60 A. J. Crum, P. Salovey, and S. Achor, "Rethinking Stress: The Role of Mindsets in Determining the Stress Response," *Journal of Personality and Social Psychology* 104 (2013): 716–33.

61 M. J. Poulin, E. A. Holman, and A. Buffone, "The Neurogenetics of Nice: Receptor Genes for Oxytocin and Vasopressin Interact with Threat to Predict Prosocial Behavior," *Psychological Science* 23 (2012): 446–52.

62 J. Segal, *Winning Life's Toughest Battles* (New York: McGraw-Hill, 1986); R. B. Brooks and S. Goldstein, *Raising Resilient Children: Fostering Strength, Hope, and Optimism in Your Child* (Lincolnwood, IL: Contemporary Books, 2001).

63 Ö. Ayduk and E. Kross, "Analyzing Negative Experiences Without Ruminating: The Role of Self-Distancing in Enabling Adaptive Self-Reflection," *Social and Personality Psychology Compass* 4 (2010): 841–54; E. Kross, A. Duckworth, Ö. Ayduk, Eli Tsukayama, and W. Mischel, "The Effect of Self-Distancing on Adaptive versus Maladaptive Self-reflection in Children," *Emotion* 11 (2011): 1032–9; W. Mischel, *The Marshmallow Test*.

64 E. Kross, E. Bruehlman-Senecal, J. Park, A. Burson, A. Daugherty, and J. Moser. "Self-Talk as a Regulatory Mechanism: How You Do It Matters," *Journal of Personality and Social Psychology* 106 (2014): 304–324.

65 Poulin, Holman, and Buffone, "The Neurogenetics of Nice" (2012); K. McGonigal, *The Upside of Stress: Why Stress Is Good for You, and How to Get Good at It* (New York: Penguin, 2016).

Activity 22

66 M. J. Meaney, "Maternal Care, Gene Expression, and the Transmission of Individual Differences in Stress Reactivity across Generations," *Annual Review of Neuroscience* 24 (2001): 1161–92; P. Tough, *How Children Succeed: Grit, Curiosity, and the Hidden Power of Character* (Boston, MA: Houghton Mifflin Harcourt, 2012).

67 Brooks and Goldstein, *Raising Resilient Children* (2001); Segal, *Winning Life's Toughest Battles* (1986).

68 G. M. Walton and G. L. Cohen, "A Brief Social-Belonging Intervention Improves Academic and Health Outcomes of Minority Students," *Science* 331 (2011): 1447–51.

69 S. Achor, *The Happiness Advantage* (New York: Random House, 2010); G. Rizzolatti and L. Craighero, "The Mirror-Neuron System," *Annual Review of Neuroscience* 27 (2004): 169–92.

Activity 23

70 A. L. Duckworth and D. S. Yeager, "Measurement Matters: Assessing Personal Qualities Other Than Cognitive Ability for Educational Purposes," *Educational Researcher* 44 (2015): 237–51.

Caren Baruch-Feldman, PhD, is a clinical psychologist and a certified school psychologist. She maintains a private practice in Scarsdale, NY, and works as a school psychologist in Harrison, NY. Baruch-Feldman has authored numerous articles and led workshops on topics such as cognitive behavioral therapy (CBT) techniques, helping children and adults cope with stress and worry, helping people change, and developing grit and self-control. She is a fellow and supervisor in rational emotive behavior therapy (REBT), a type of CBT. Visit her online at www.drbaruchfeldman.com.

Foreword writer **Thomas R. Hoerr, PhD**, is emeritus head of New City Schools, and scholar-in-residence at University of Missouri-St. Louis. He is author of *The Formative Five*, *Fostering Grit*, and *The Art of School Leadership*.

More ⏱ Instant Help Books for Teens

GET OUT OF YOUR MIND & INTO YOUR LIFE FOR TEENS
A Guide to Living an
Extraordinary Life
ISBN: 978-1608821938 / US $15.95

OVERCOMING PROCRASTINATION FOR TEENS
A CBT Guide for
College-Bound Students
ISBN 978-1626254572 / US $16.95

THE TEEN GIRL'S SURVIVAL GUIDE
Ten Tips for Making Friends,
Avoiding Drama & Coping
with Social Stress
ISBN: 978-1626253063 / US $16.95

THE PERFECTIONISM WORKBOOK FOR TEENS
Activities to Help You Reduce
Anxiety & Get Things Done
ISBN 978-1626254541 / US $16.95

THE SELF-ESTEEM WORKBOOK FOR TEENS
Activities to Help You Build
Confidence & Achieve Your Goals
ISBN 978-1608825820 / US $15.95

COMMUNICATION SKILLS FOR TEENS
How to Listen, Express &
Connect for Success
ISBN: 978-1626252639 / US $16.95

Register your **new harbinger** titles for additional benefits!

When you register your **new harbinger** title—purchased in any format, from any source—you get access to benefits like the following:

- Downloadable accessories like printable worksheets and extra content

- Instructional videos and audio files

- Information about updates, corrections, and new editions

Not every title has accessories, but we're adding new material all the time.

Access free accessories in 3 easy steps:

1. Sign in at NewHarbinger.com (or **register** to create an account).

2. Click on **register a book**. Search for your title and click the **register** button when it appears.

3. Click on the **book cover or title** to go to its details page. Click on **accessories** to view and access files.

That's all there is to it!

If you need help, visit:

NewHarbinger.com/accessories

new harbinger
CELEBRATING
40 YEARS